Life: An Abuser's Manual

Life:
An Abuser's
Manual

Matthew Kemp

Michael O'Mara Books Limited

First published in Great Britain in 1999
by Michael O'Mara Books Limited
9 Lion Yard
Tremadoc Road
London SW4 7NQ

Life: An Abuser's Manual is published under licence from Paperlink Ltd
356 Kennington Road, London SE11 4LD.
Copyright © Paperlink Ltd 1999.

All rights reserved. No part of this publication may be reproduced,
stored in a retrieval system, or transmitted by any means,
without the prior permission in writing of the publisher,
nor be otherwise circulated in any form of binding or cover
other than that in which it is published and without a similar
condition including this condition being imposed on the
subsequent purchaser.

The right of Matthew Kemp to be identified as the author of
this work has been asserted by him in accordance with
the Copyright, Designs and Patents Act 1988.

A CIP catalogue record for this book is available from
the British Library

ISBN 1-85479-465-5

1 3 5 7 9 10 8 6 4 2

Designed by Mick Keates
Formatting by Concise Artisans
Printed and bound in Great Britain by
Cox & Wyman Ltd, Reading, Berks.

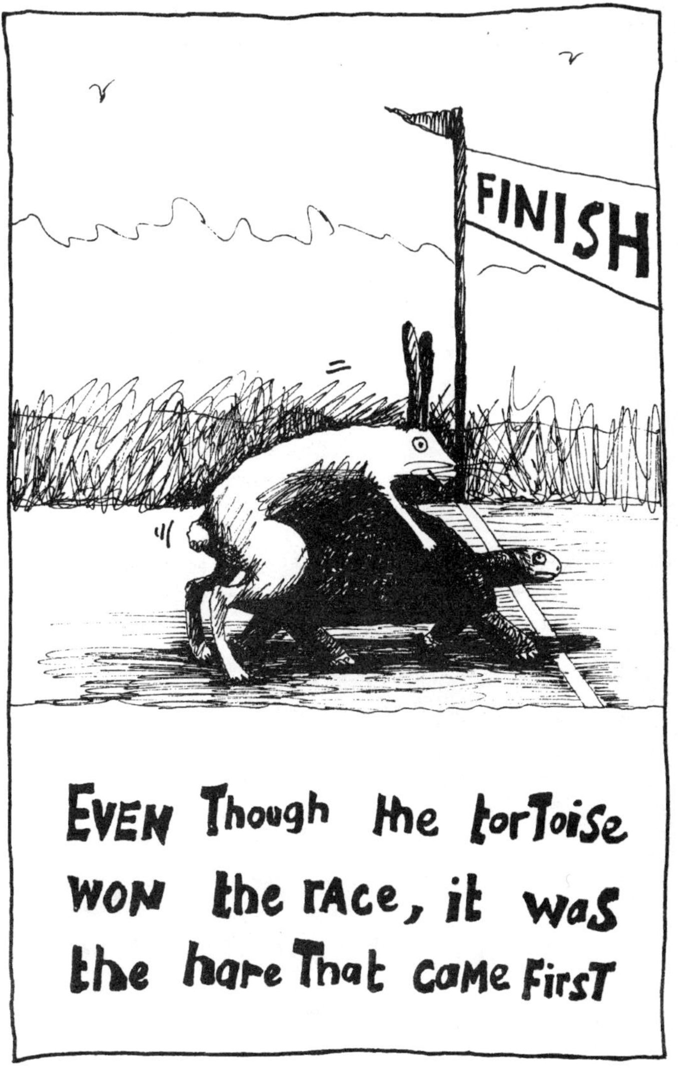
FINISH

EVEN Though the tortoise won the race, it was the hare That came First

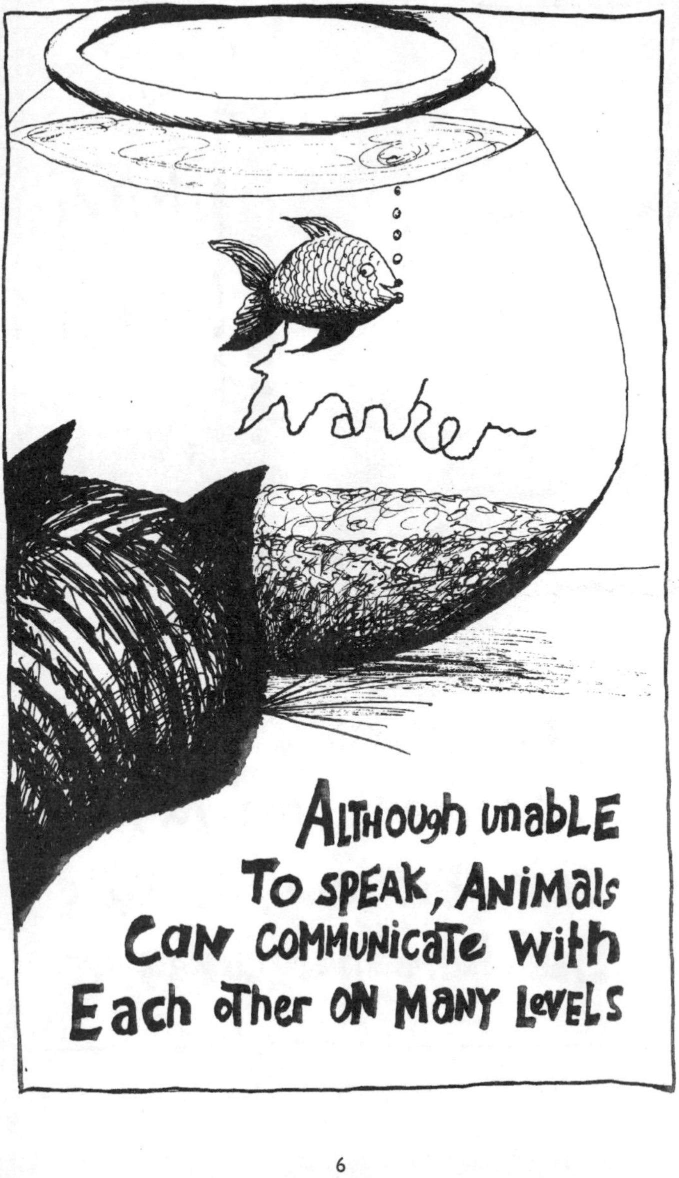
wanker
ALTHOUGH UNABLE
TO SPEAK, ANIMALS
CAN COMMUNICATE WITH
EACH OTHER ON MANY LEVELS

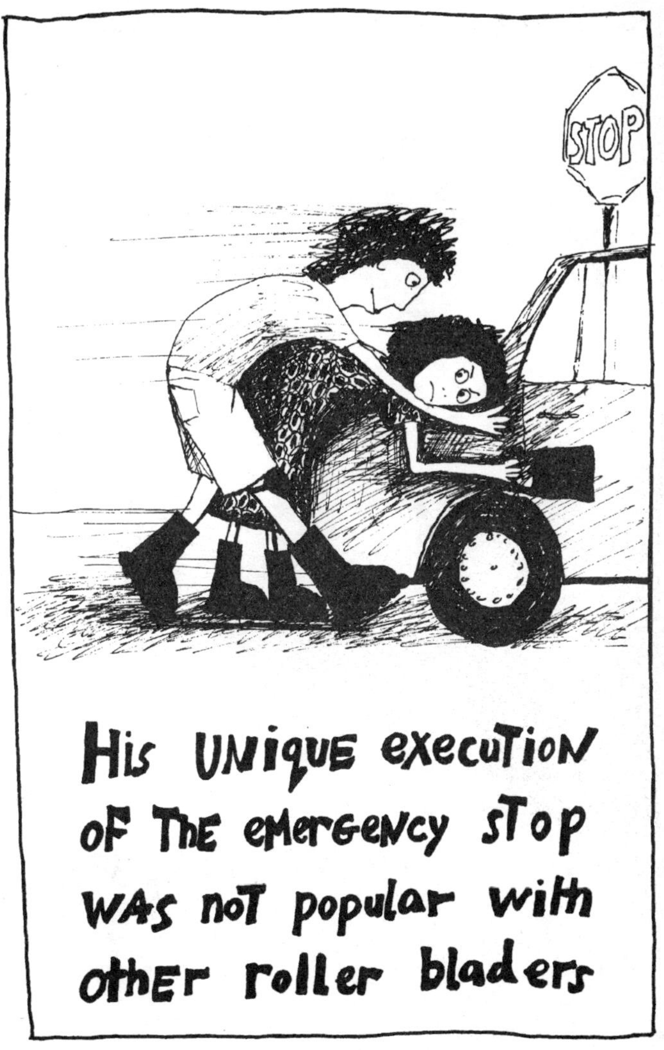
STOP

His UNIQUE execution of The emergency sTop WAS noT popular with other roller bladers

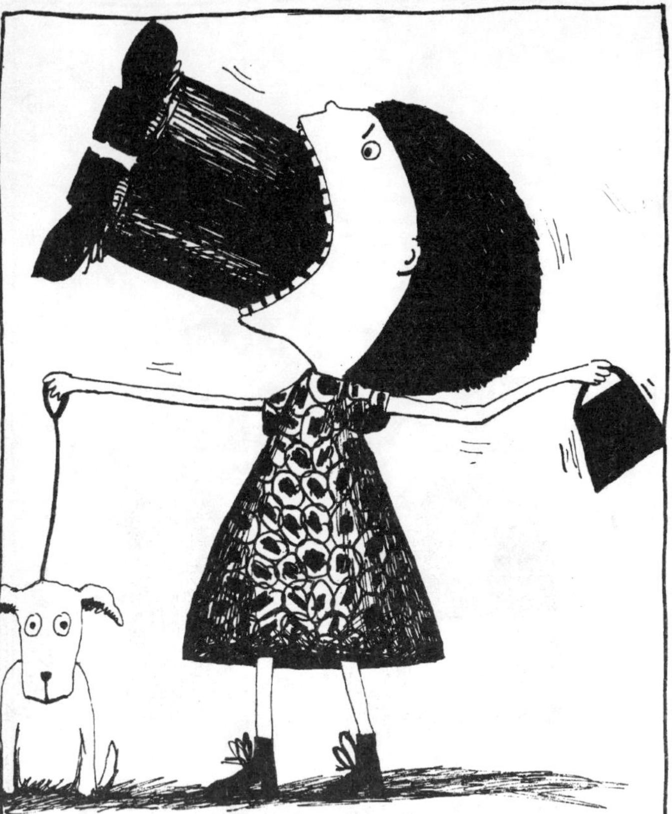

His Attempt At Snogging Her in the park coincided with one of Her unpredictably violent mood swings

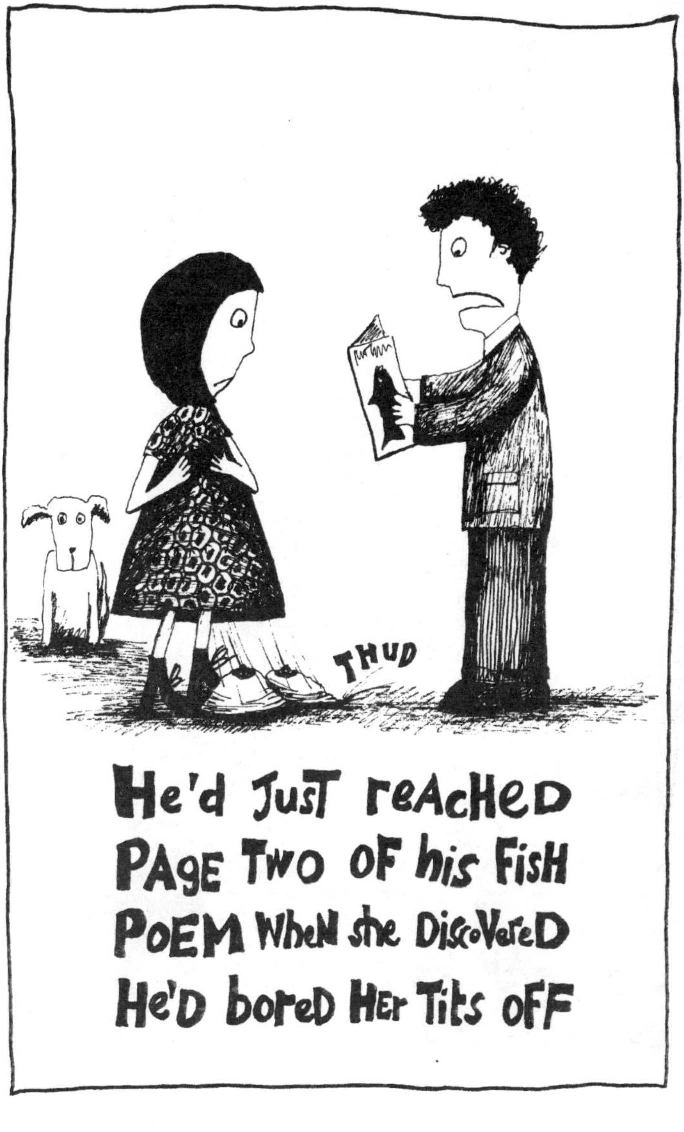
THUD
He'd Just reached PAGE TWO OF his FisH POEM when she DiscoVereD He'D bored Her Tits oFF

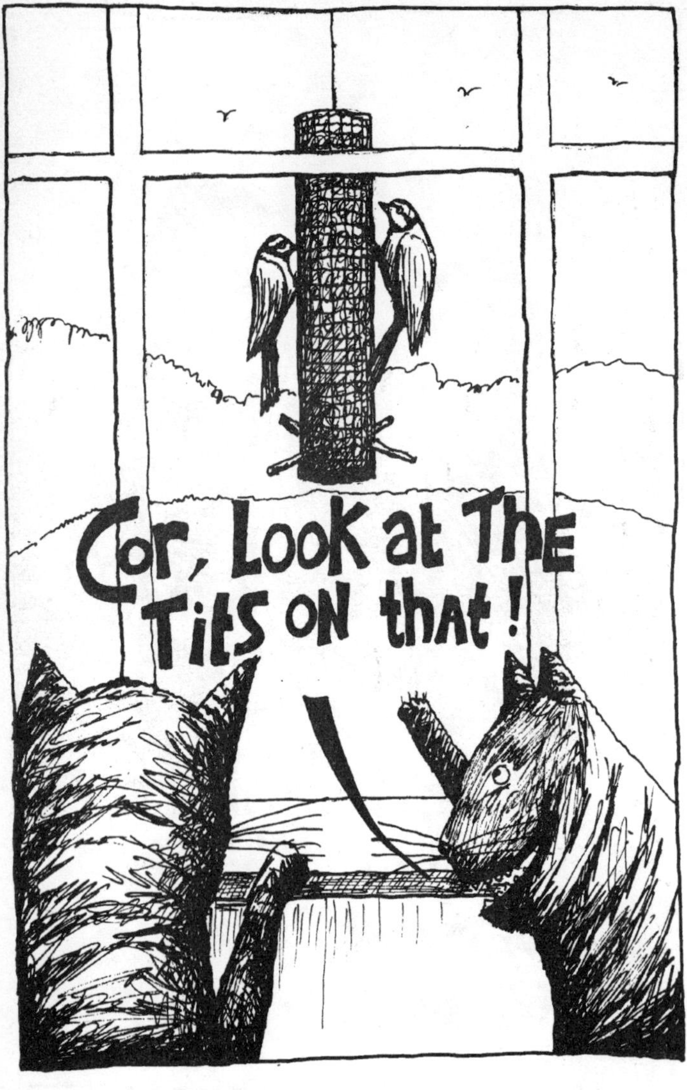
Cor, Look at The Tits ON that!

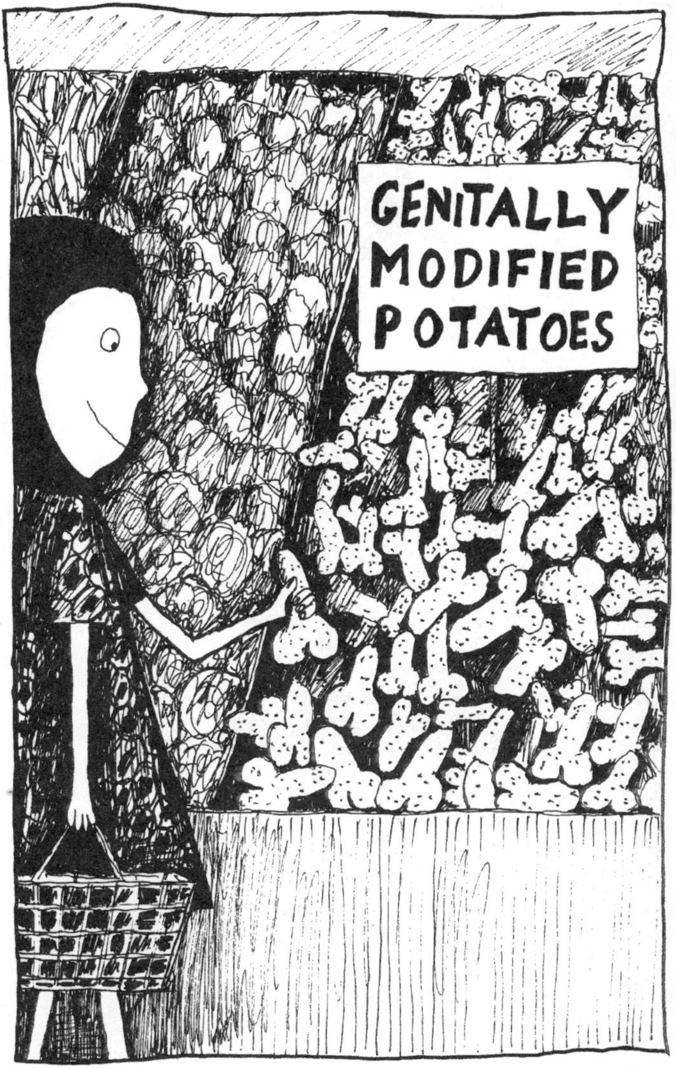
GENITALLY
MODIFIED
POTATOES

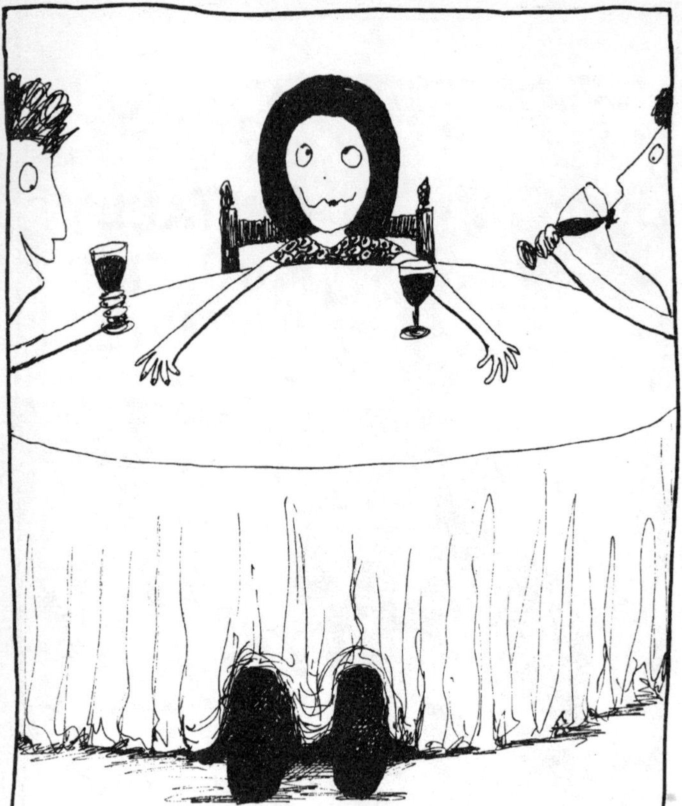

He FOUND the subject of oral sex went down well AT Dinner Parties

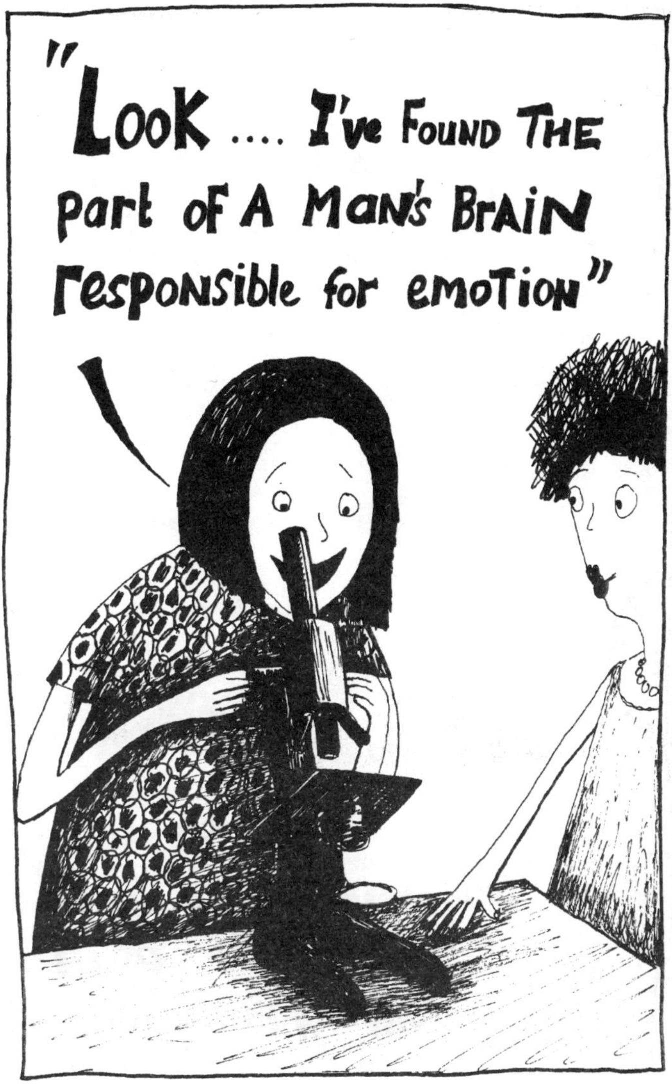
"LOOK .... I've FOUND THE part of A Man's BrAIN responsible for emotion"

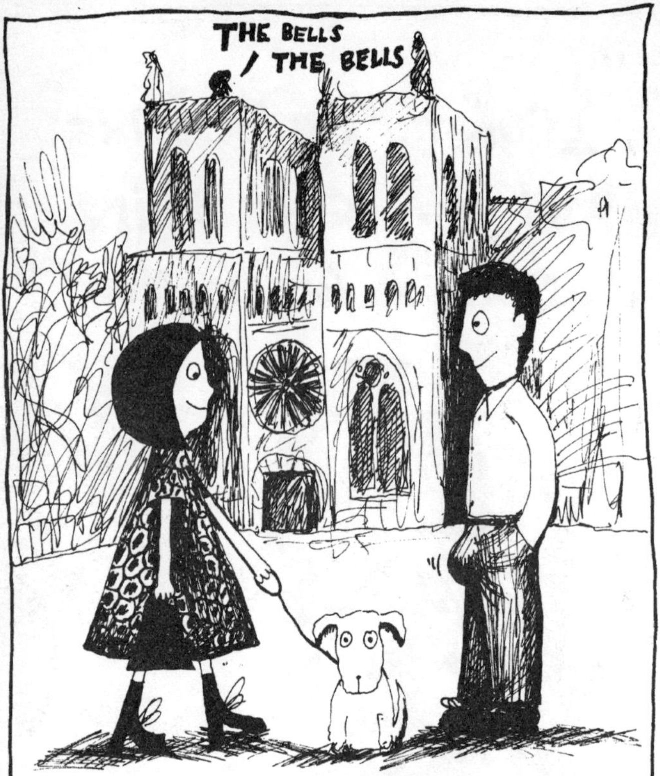
THE BELLS / THE BELLS

Known as 'The Lunch pack of Notre Dame', Quasimodo's Brother was a Much Bigger Hit with the Girls

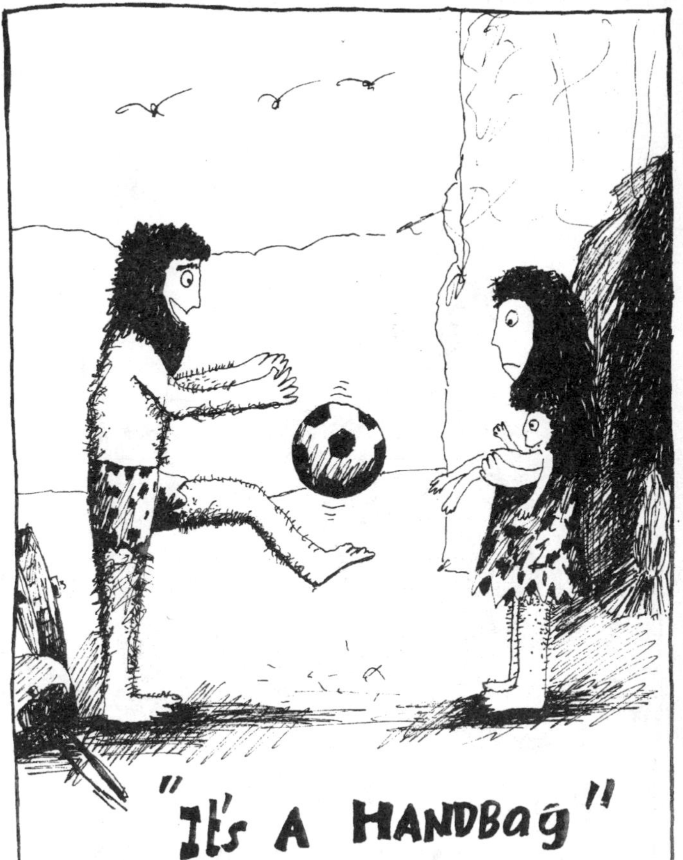

"It's A HANDBag"
HE SAID, trying to
CONVINCE Her He'D InventeD
SOMEThing USEFUL

She was more into peeping
at Peter Piper's pack of
pickled peppers than selling
silly sea shells on the sea shore

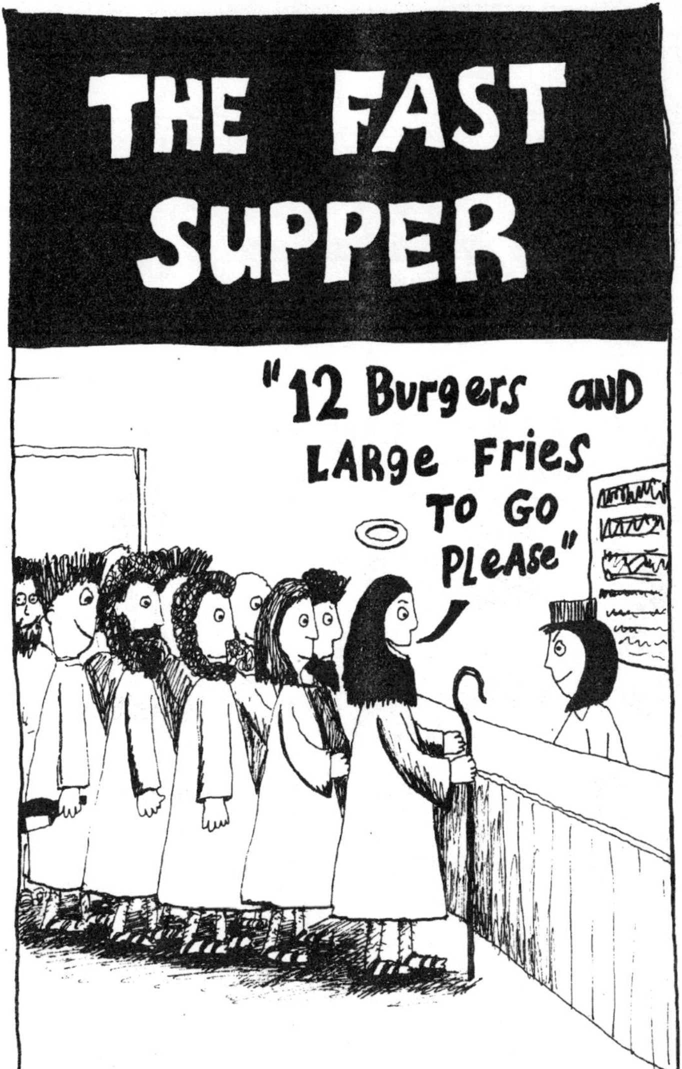
THE FAST SUPPER
"12 Burgers aND LARge Fries TO GO PLeAse"

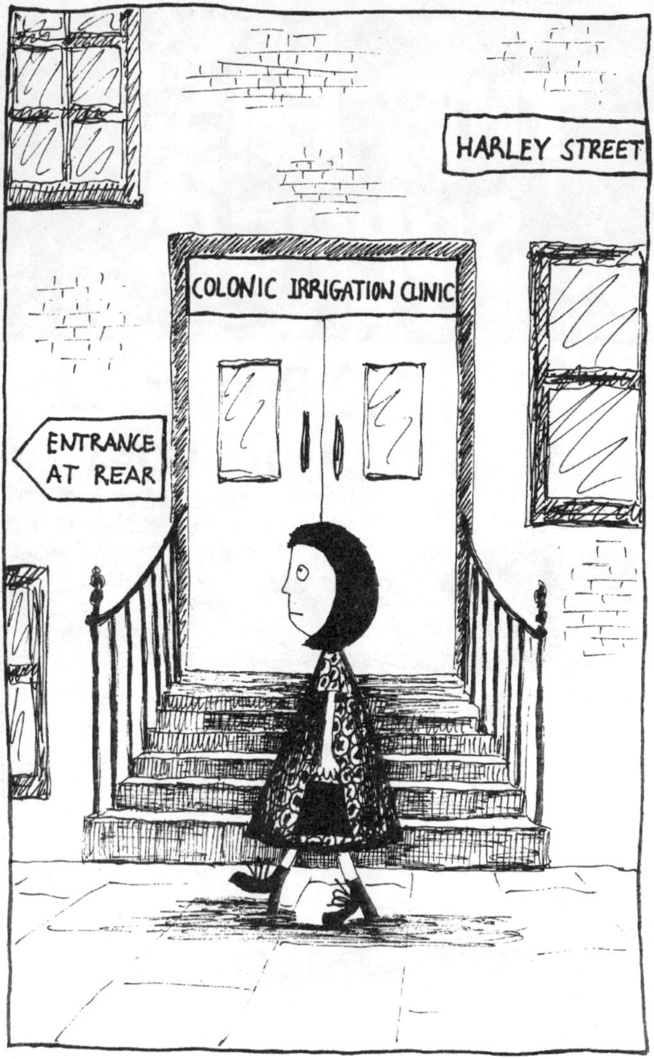
HARLEY STREET
COLONIC IRRIGATION CLINIC
ENTRANCE
AT REAR

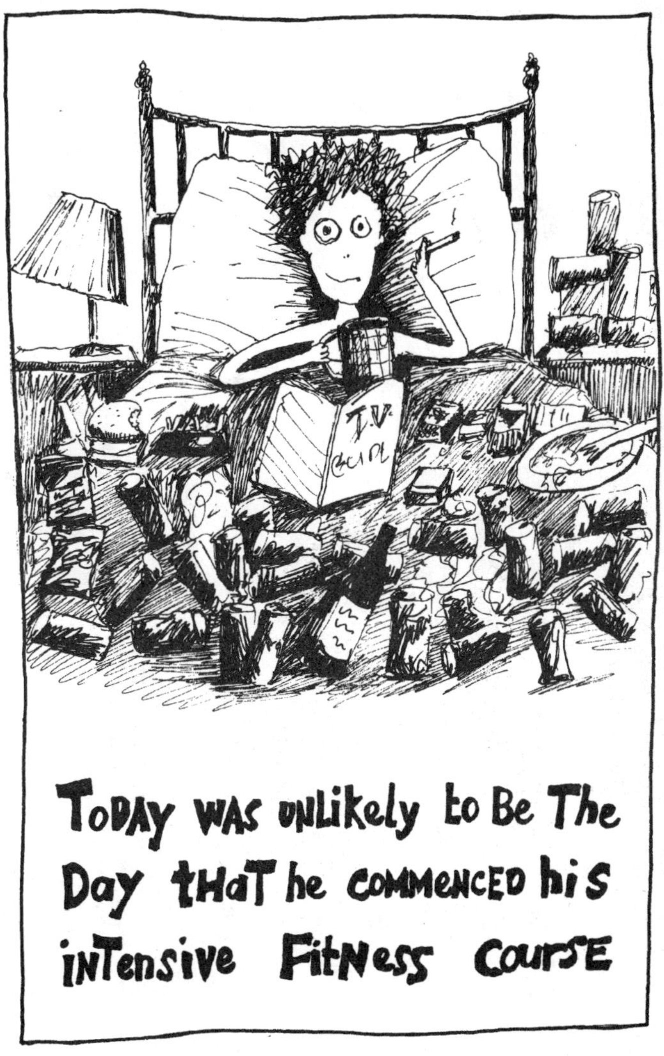
T.V.
GUIDE

Today was unlikely to be the day that he commenced his intensive fitness course

"Hello Room service, CAN you SEND Me A DISH with more Meat on it?
A Small detail WASN'T going To spoil The Birthday Night of Her Dreams

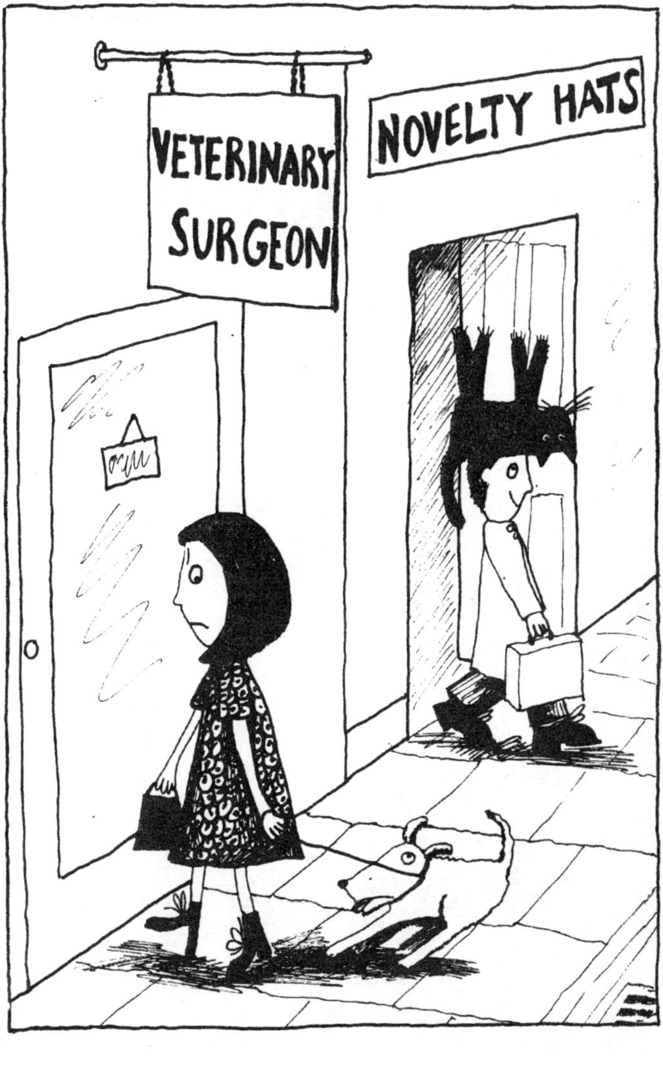
VETERINARY SURGEON
NOVELTY HATS

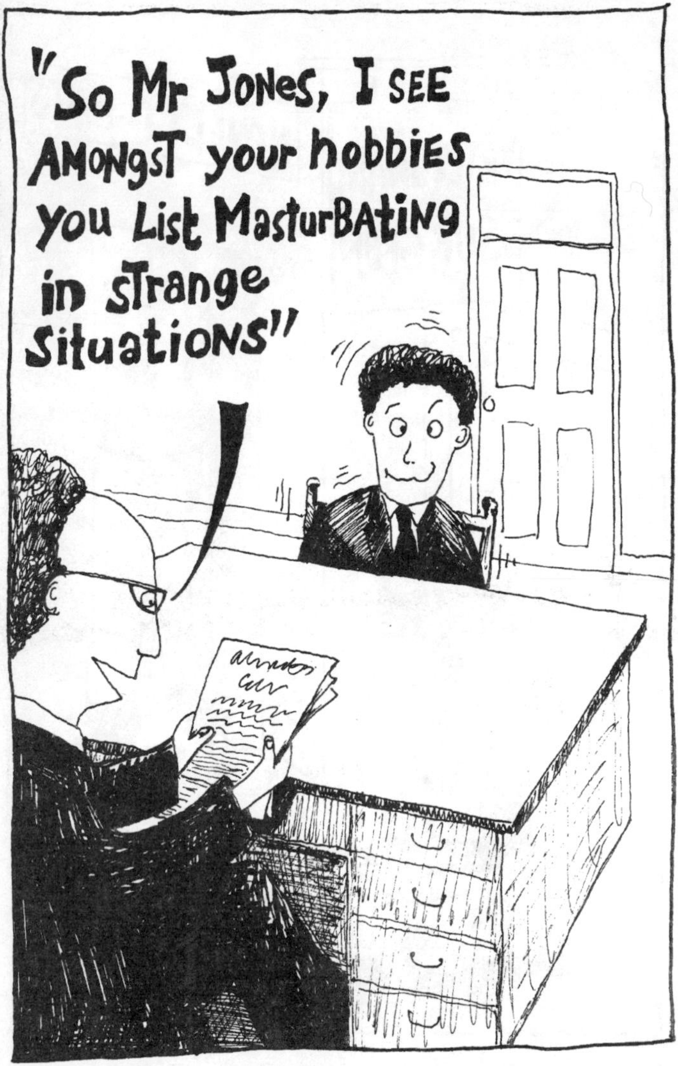
"So Mr Jones, I SEE AMONGST your hobbies you List MasturBATING in STrange Situations"

Any patient facing
one of Dr Lovestein's
rectal exams MADE
a REMARKABLY
spEedy recovery

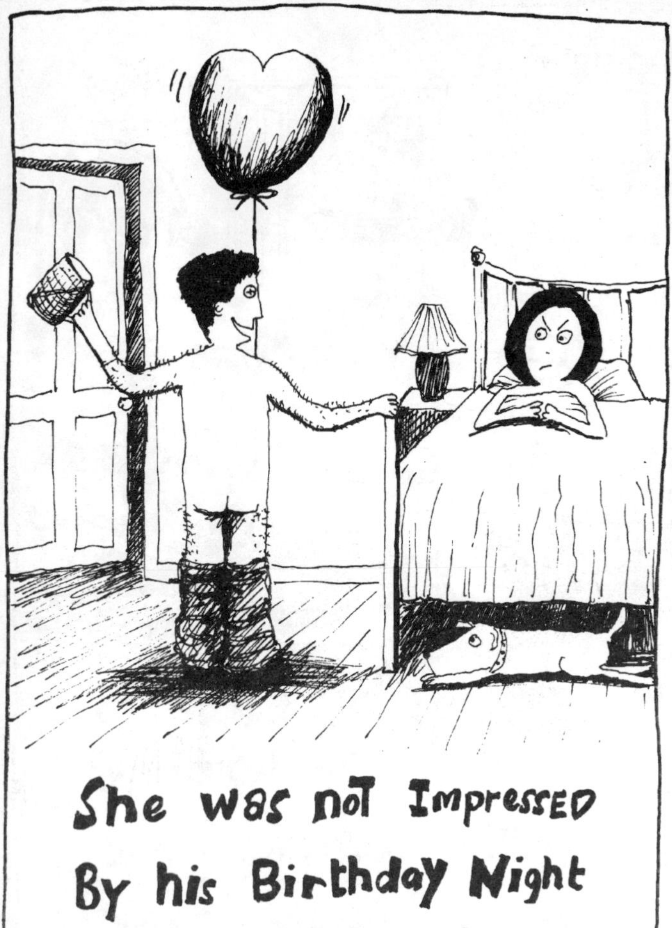
She was not Impressed
By his Birthday Night
"see, I can keep it up
after 10 pints" JOKE

YES DocTor, it's ONE of the WorST CASeS OF MediA INTrUSION I've ever SEEN

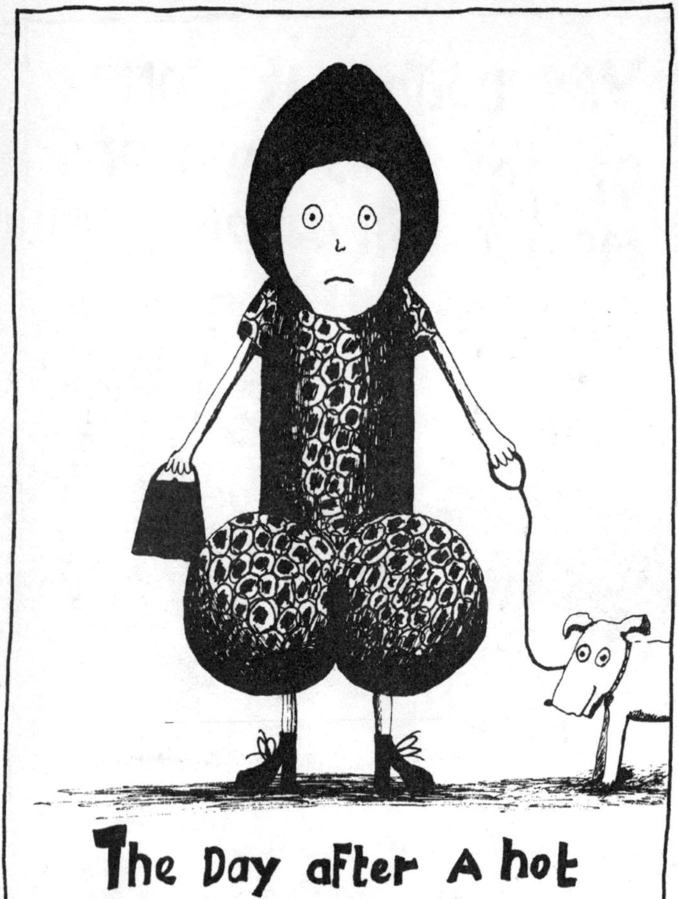

The Day after A hot DaTe is A BAD time to start Believing You are What you EAT

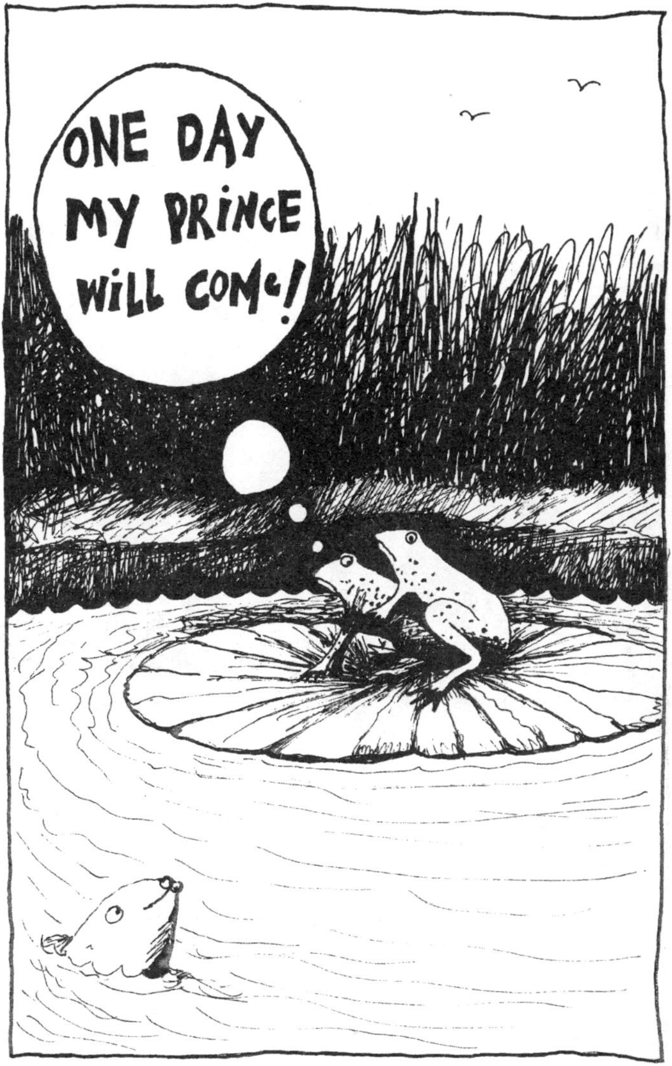
ONE DAY MY PRINCE WILL COME!

THE DOCTOR WAS NOT
FOOLED by His 'It
SLIPPED while I WAS
CLEANING My Trousers' STORY

A SOMEWHAT SEVERE
CASE OF CRABS NIPPED
HIS idea OF a holiday
Romance IN THE BUD

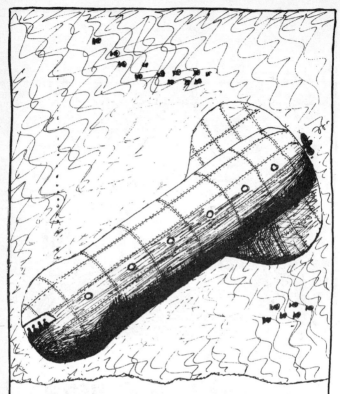

The Navy told the ship yard to build a vessel capable of taking seamen deeper than they'd ever been before

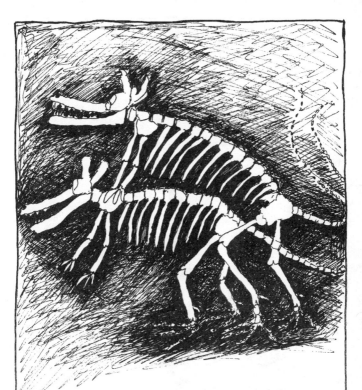

Even the valiant Efforts
of THE shaggasaurus
couldn't prevent the
extinction of the Dinosaurs

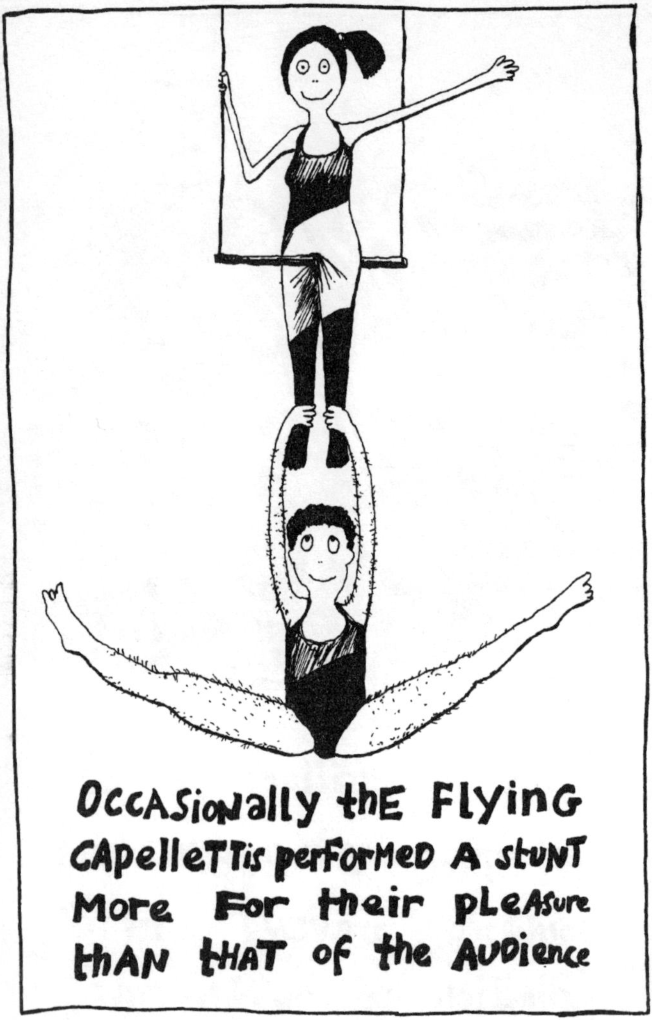
OCCASIONALLY THE FLYING
CAPELLETTIS PERFORMED A STUNT
MORE FOR THEIR PLEASURE
THAN THAT OF THE AUDIENCE

LAST year They celebrATed
with A Night at THE
operA And DiNNeR AT
LA GAvroche; This year
They goT bAcK to BASicS

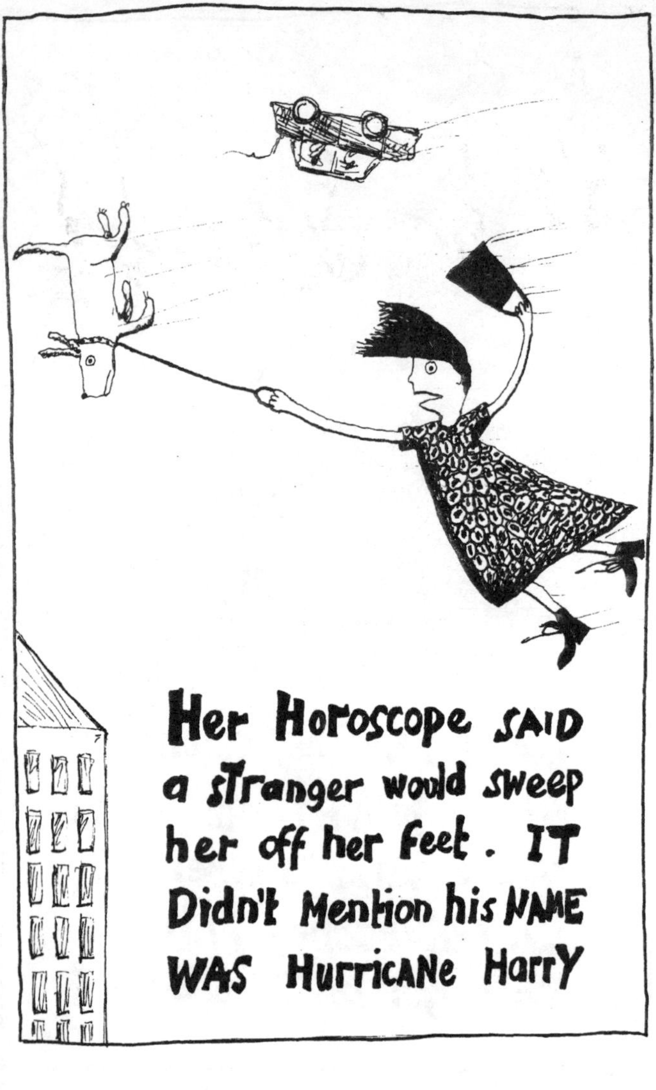
Her Horoscope SAID
a sTranger would sweep
her off her feet. IT
Didn't Mention his NAME
WAS Hurricane Harry

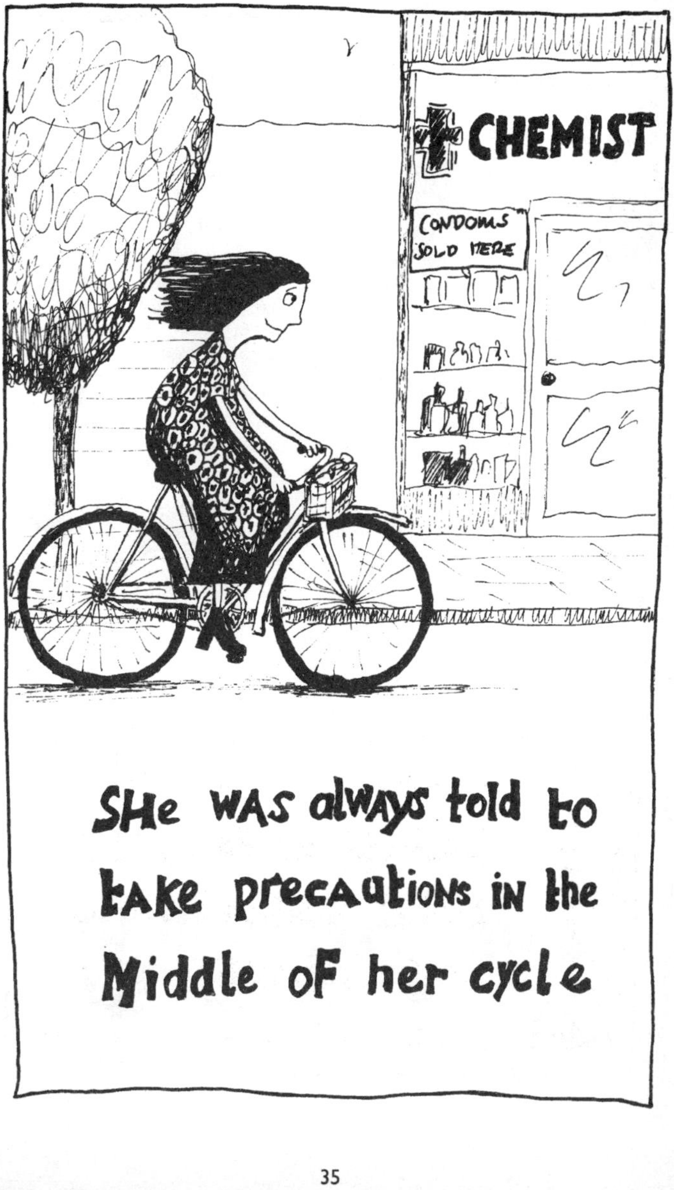
CHEMIST
CONDOMS
SOLD HERE

SHe WAS always told to take precautions in the Middle of her cycle

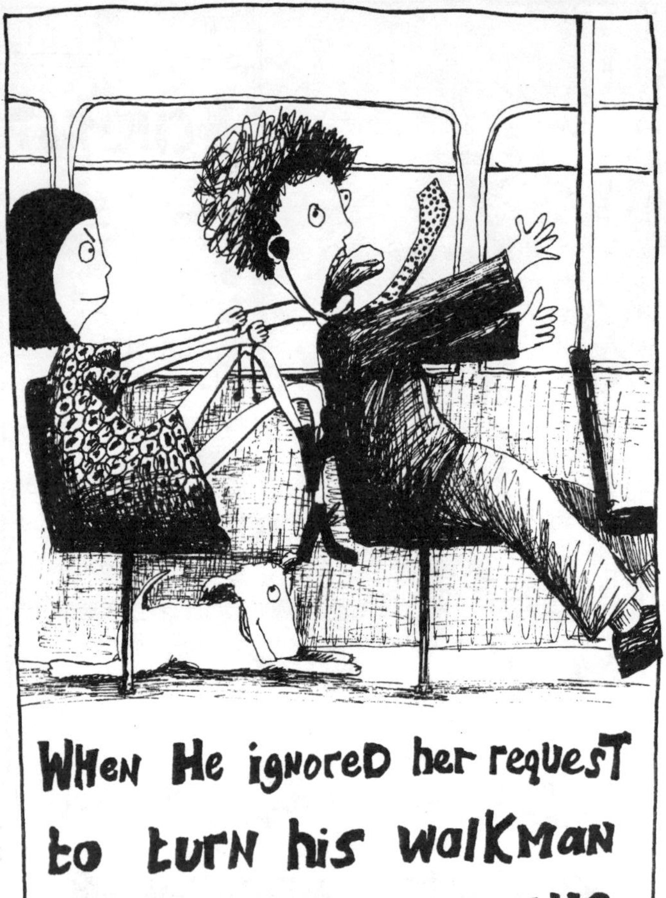
WHEN HE IGNORED HER REQUEST TO TURN HIS WALKMAN DOWN, SHE TOOK THE LAW INTO HER OWN HANDS

Her Last Minute DASH
For the Bus WAS
aided by Her New
WINGED PANTY Liners

He regretted NOT KNOWING About Rosa's passion For erotic DANCiNG BEFore introducing Her to His ParENTs

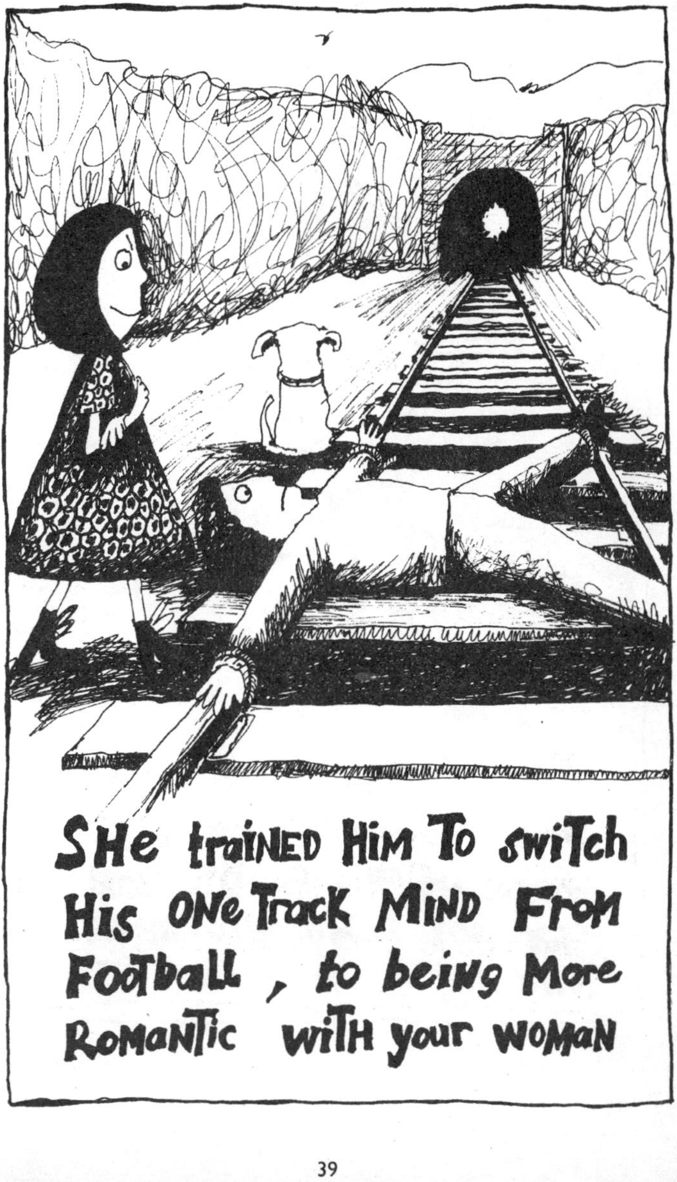

SHe trained Him To switch His ONe Track MiND From Football , to being More RoMantic with your woman

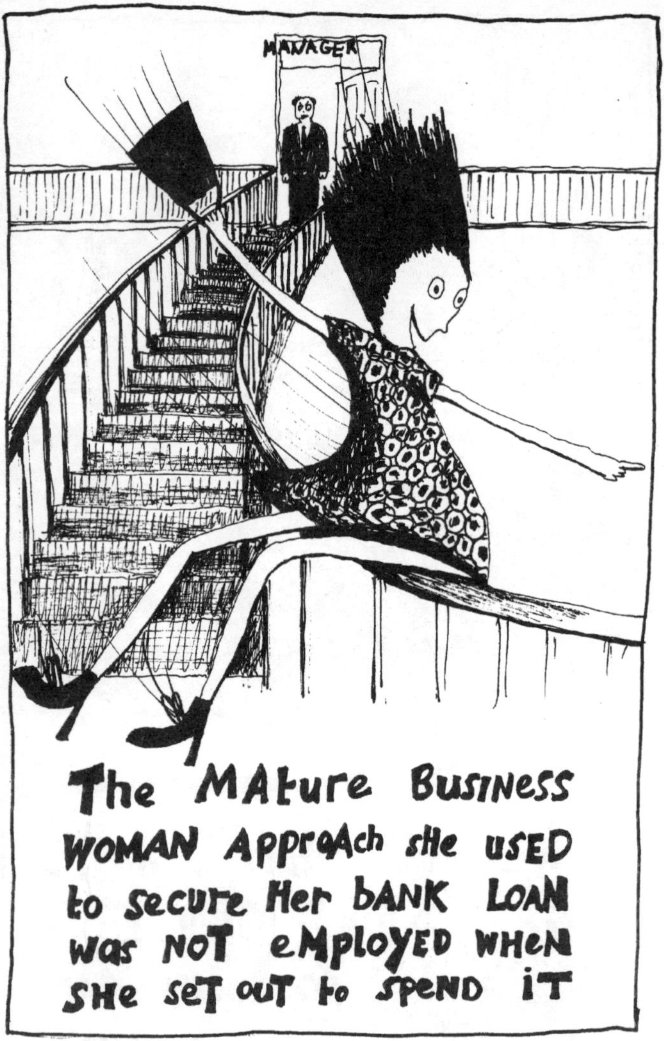
MANAGER
The MAture Business WOMAN Approach she USED to secure Her bANK LOAN was NOT eMployED WHeN SHe seT out to spend IT

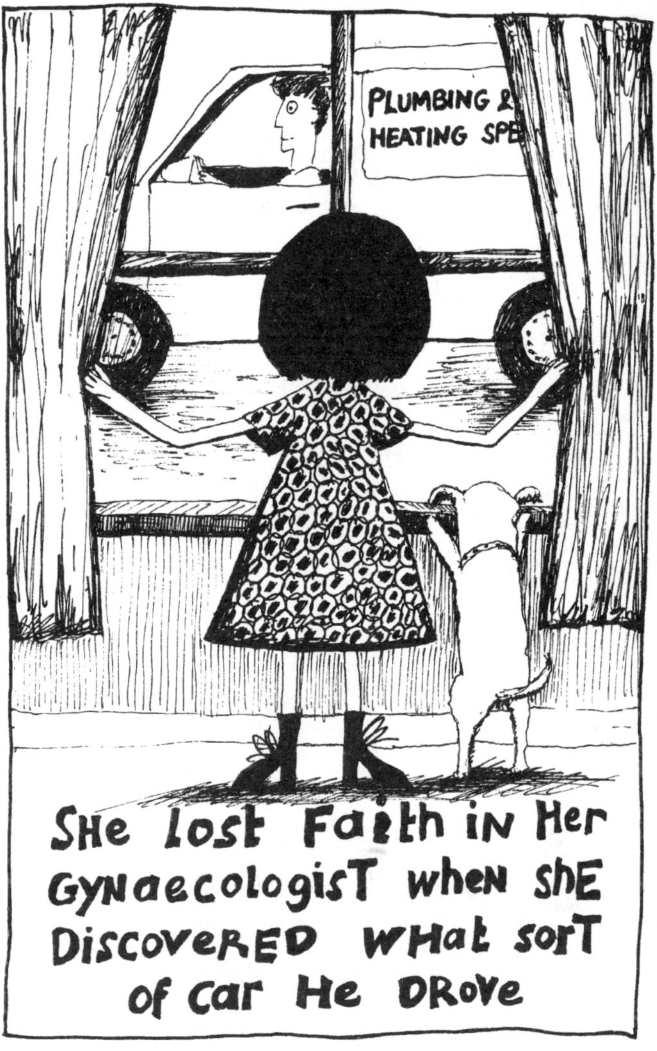
PLUMBING &
HEATING SPE

SHE lost Faith in Her GYNaecologisT when ShE DiscoveRED WHat sorT of car He DRove

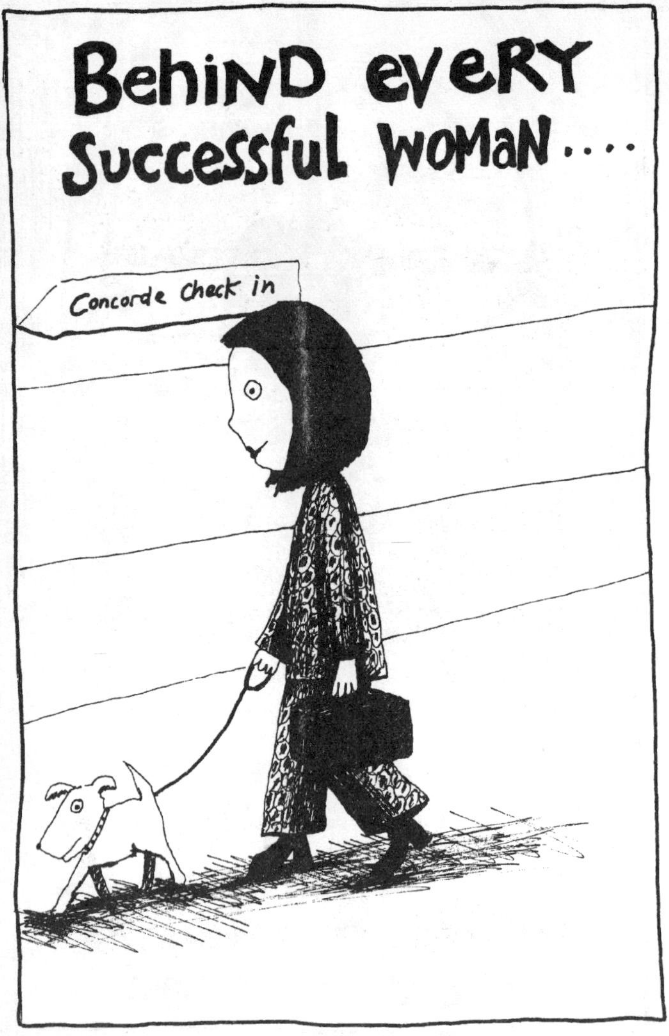
BEHIND EVERY
SUCCESSFUL WOMAN....
Concorde check in

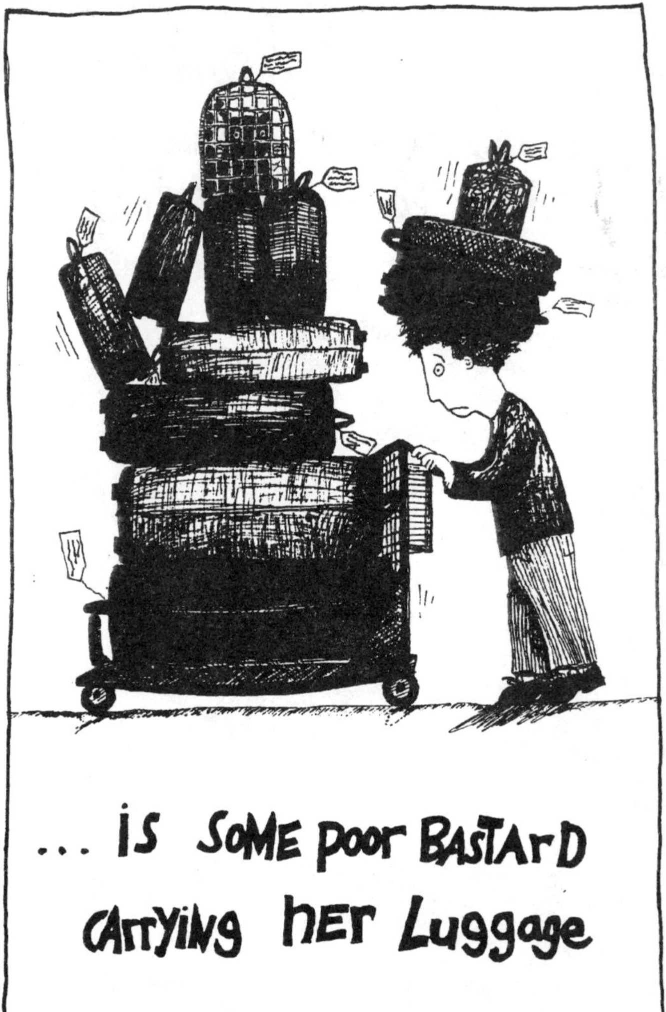
... is SOME poor BASTArD
cArrying her Luggage

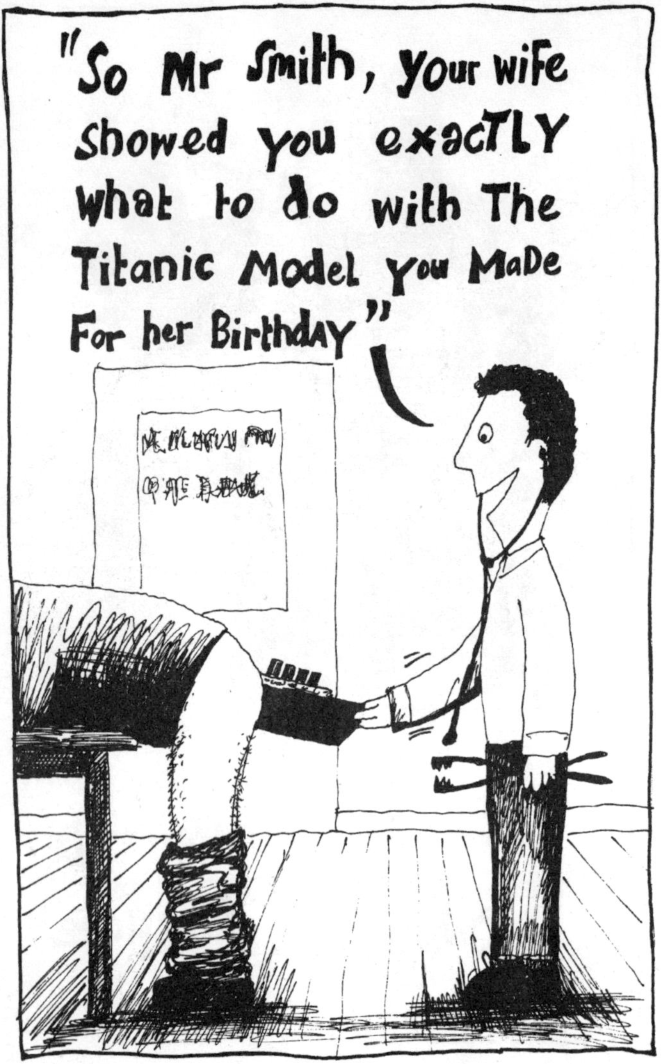
"So Mr Smith, your wife showed you exactLY what to do with The Titanic Model you MaDe For her Birthday"

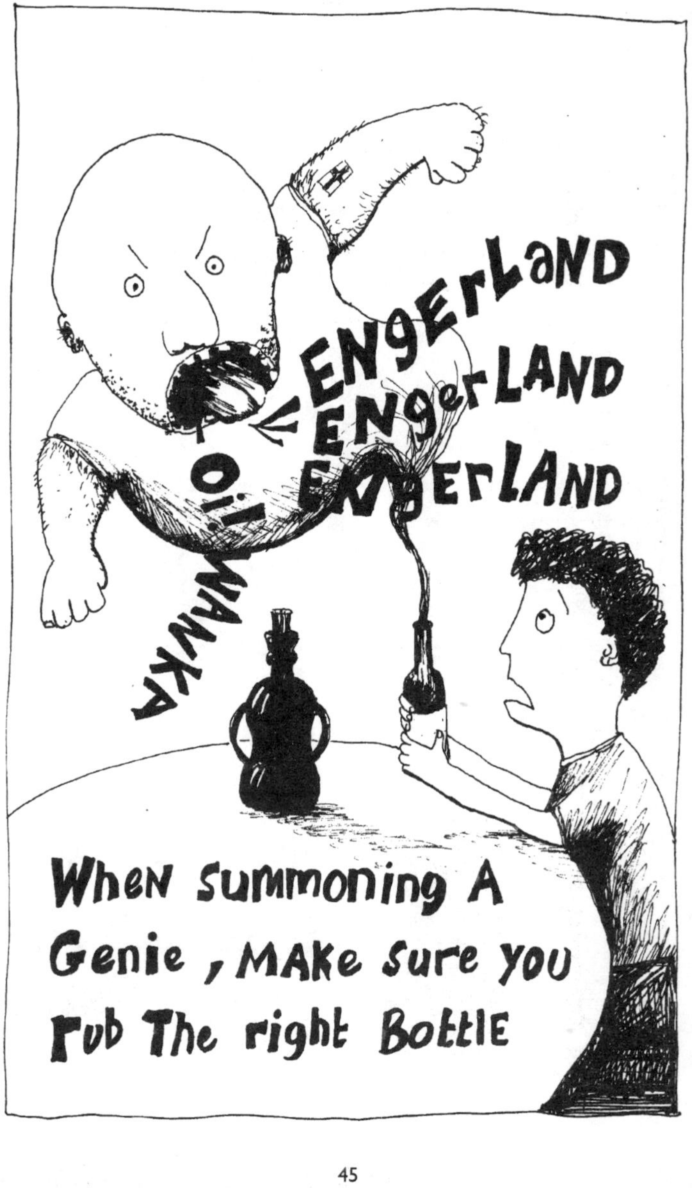
ENgerLaND
ENgerLAND
ENgerLAND
Oi! WANKA

When summoning A Genie, MAKE sure you rub The right Bottle

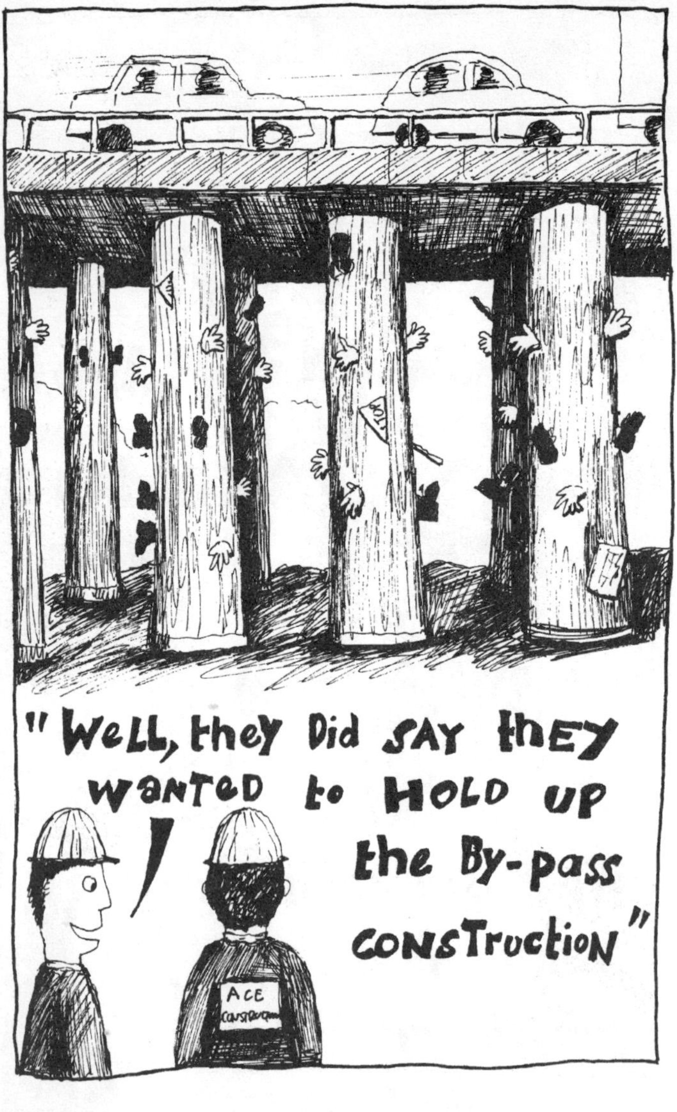
"Well, they Did SAY they wanted to HOLD UP the By-pass construction"
ACE CONSTRUCTION

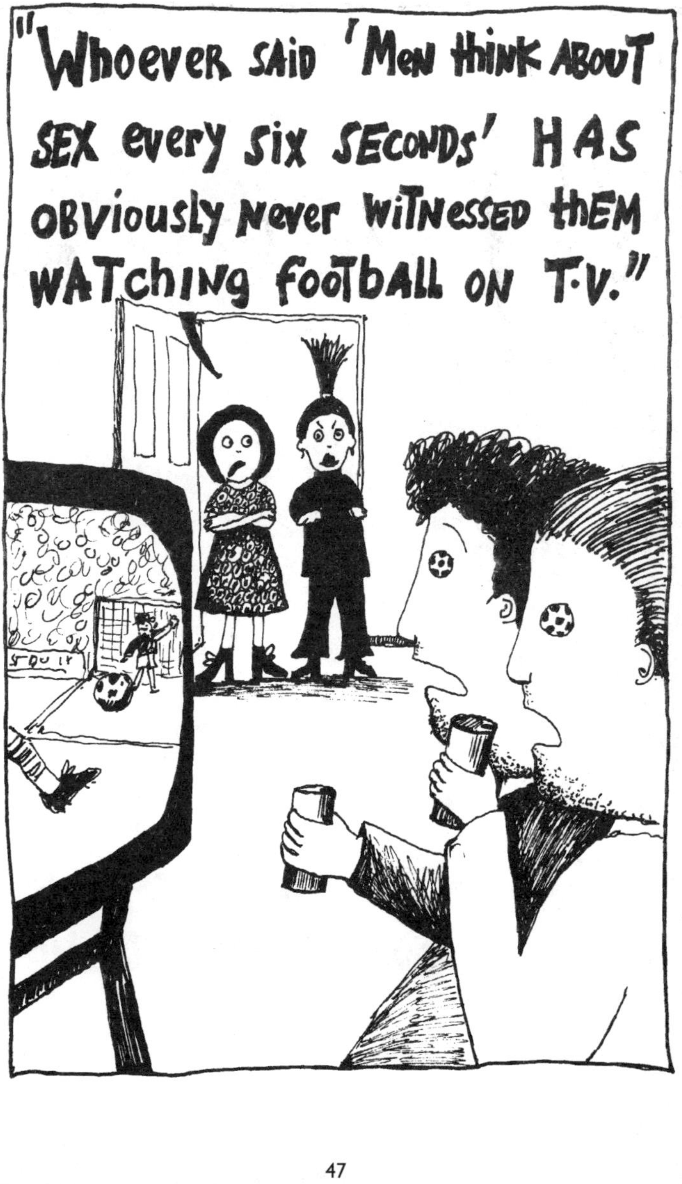
"Whoever said 'Men think about sex every six seconds' has obviously never witnessed them watching football on T.V."

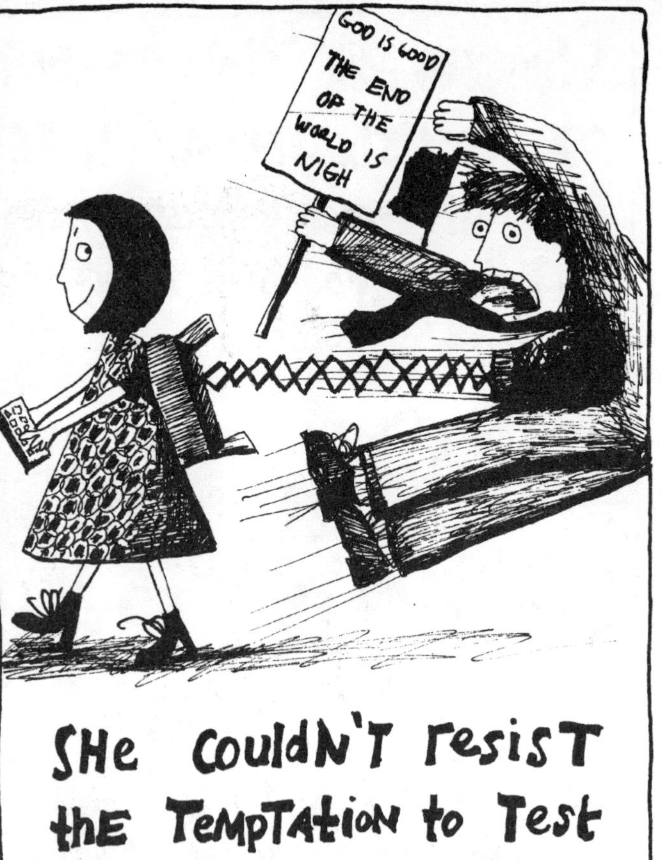
GOD IS GOOD
THE END OF THE WORLD IS NIGH

SHE COULDN'T RESIST THE TEMPTATION TO TEST THE EFFECTIVENESS OF HER NEW ANTI-ASSAULT DEVICE

THe CoNfideNCE gAiNED
FroM Her New PANTy liners
WAS UNDerMiNED by A
FAULT in Her SkirT elAStic

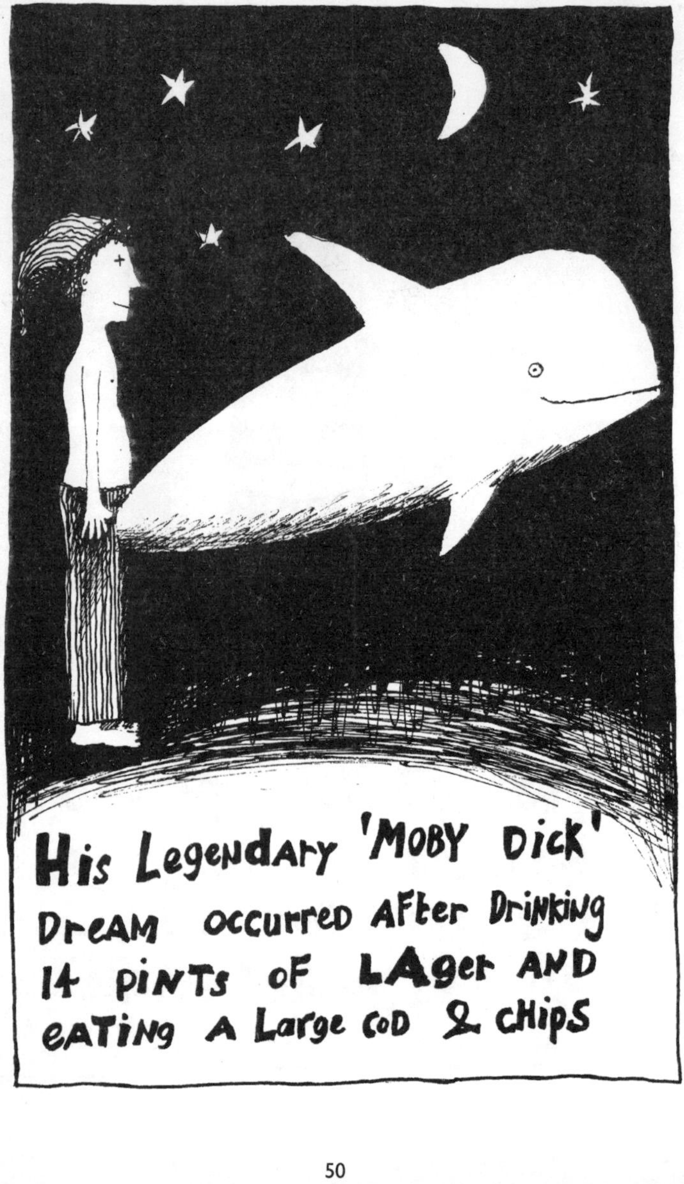
His Legendary 'MOBY DICK'
DreAM occurred After Drinking
14 piNTs oF LAger AND
eATiNg A Large coD & cHips

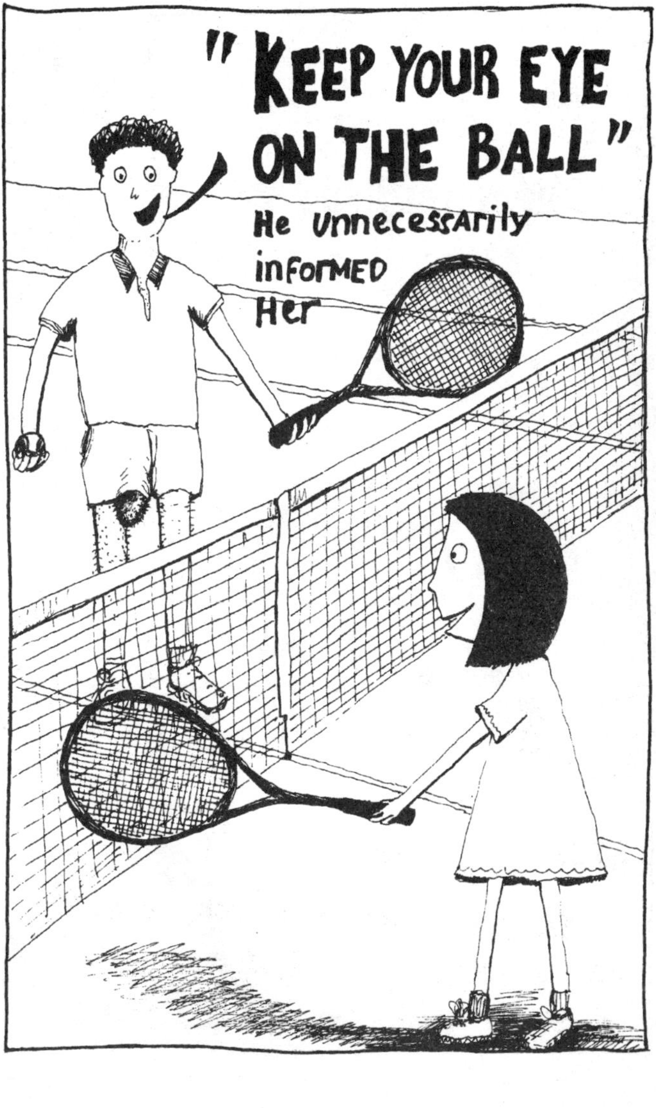
"KEEP YOUR EYE ON THE BALL"
He unnecessarily informed Her

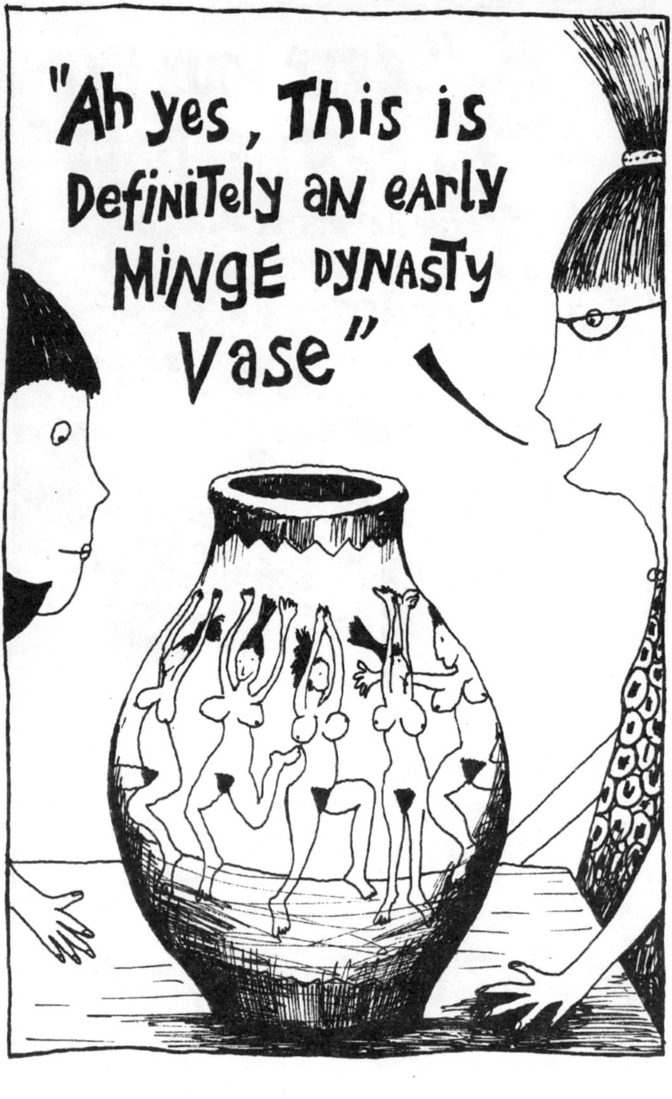
"Ah yes, This is Definitely an early MINGE DYNASTY Vase"

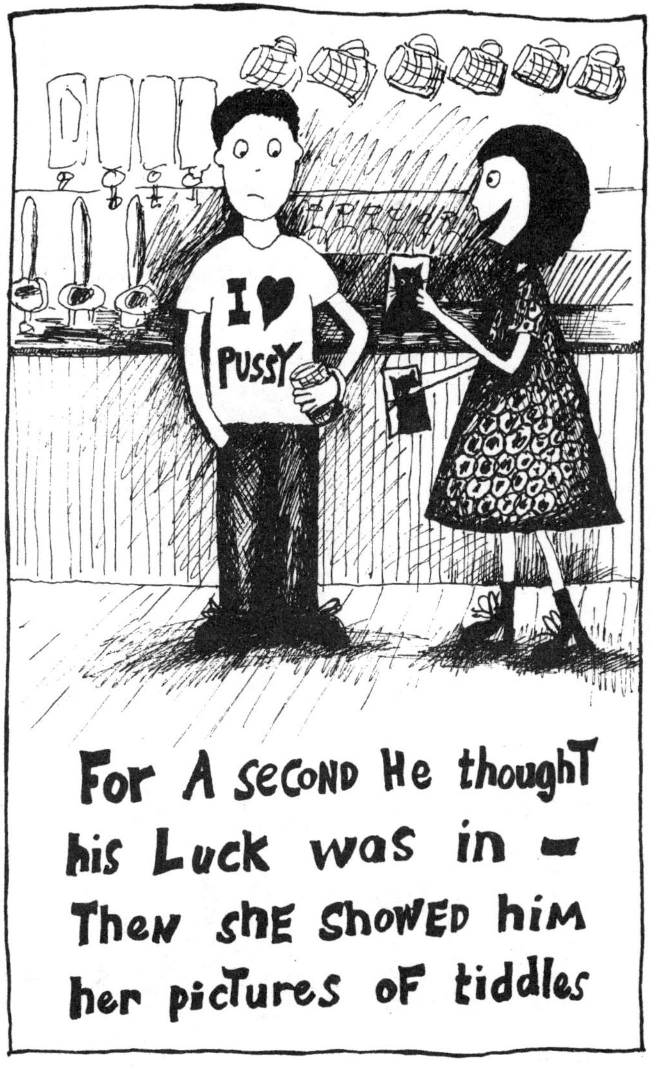
I ♥
PUSSY

For A SECOND He thoughT his Luck was in – Then SHE ShOWED him her picTures oF tiddles

The saying 'size isn't everything' MEANT little to Nellie the elephant

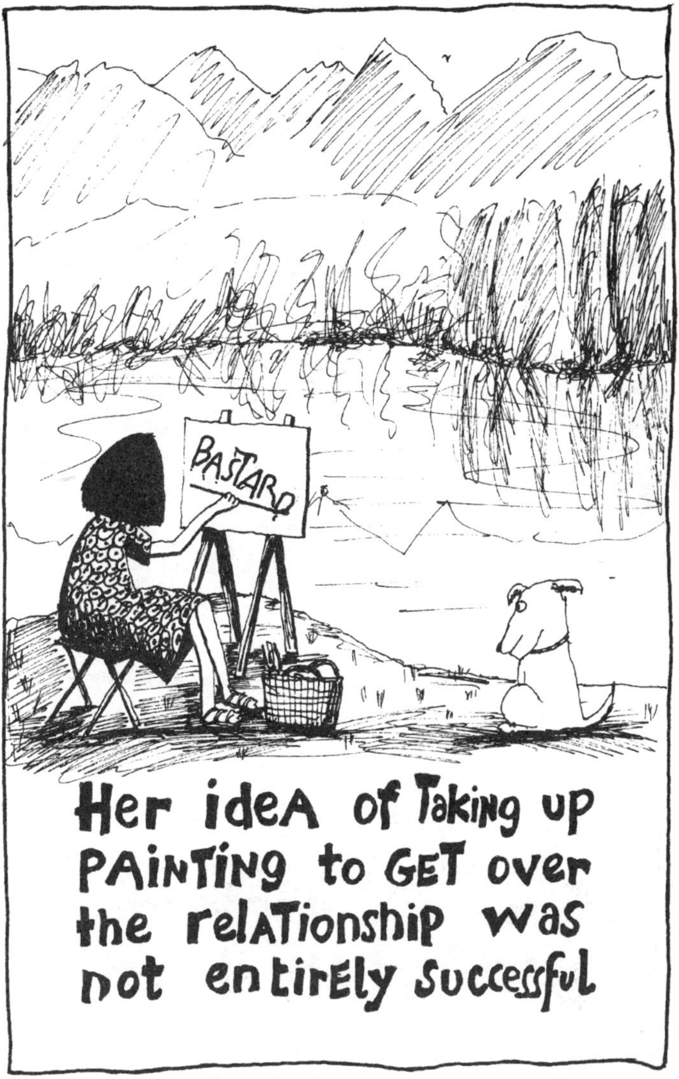
BASTARD

Her idea of Taking up PAINTING to GET over the relATionship was not entirely successful

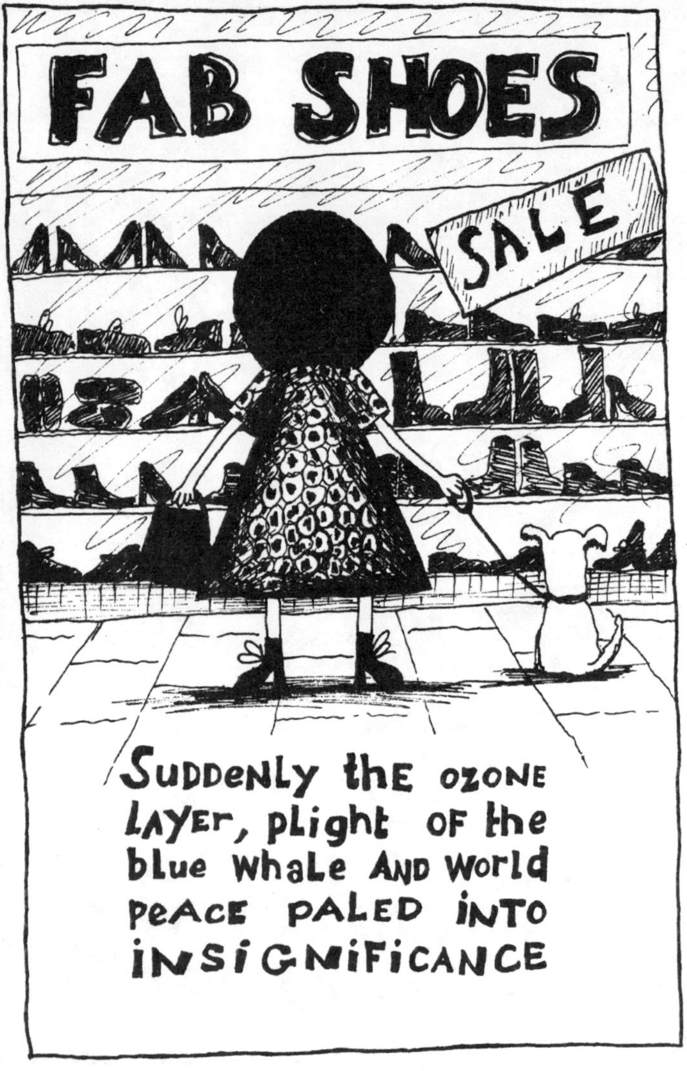
FAB SHOES
SALE
Suddenly the ozone layer, plight of the blue whale and world peace paled into insignificance

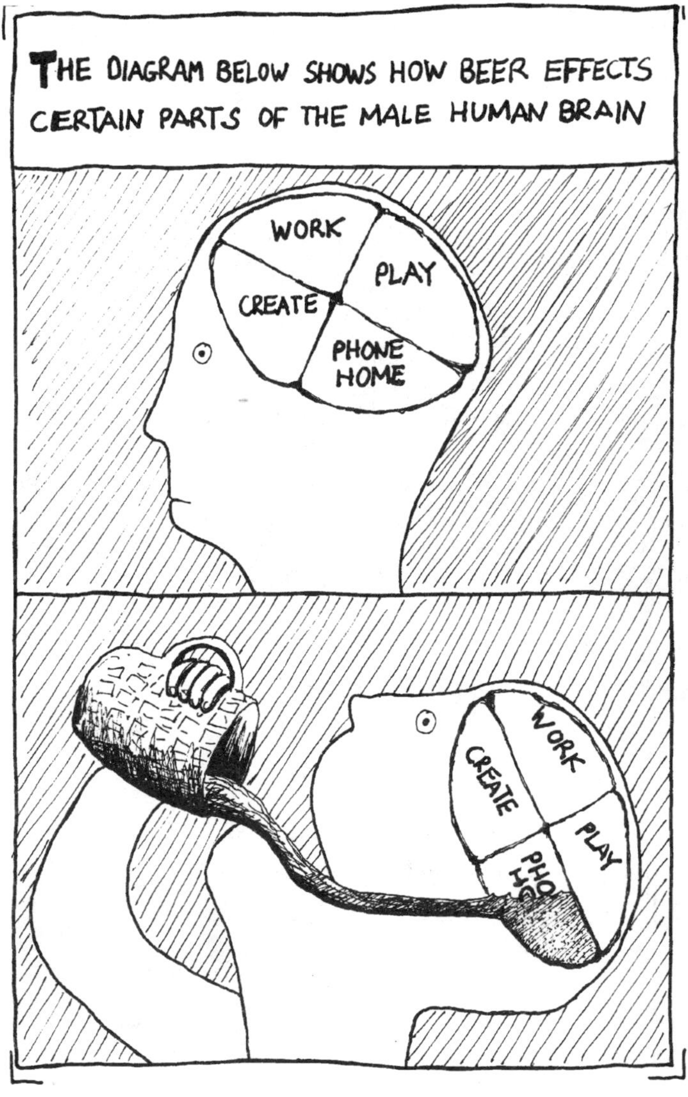
THE DIAGRAM BELOW SHOWS HOW BEER EFFECTS CERTAIN PARTS OF THE MALE HUMAN BRAIN
WORK
PLAY
CREATE
PHONE HOME
WORK
CREATE
PLAY

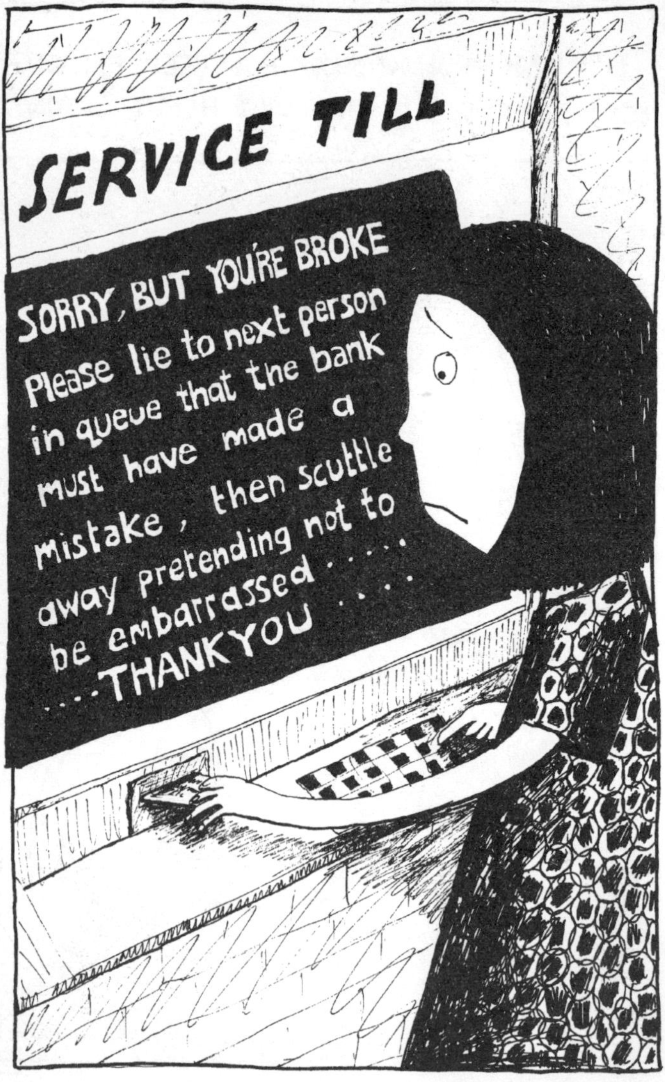
SERVICE TILL
SORRY, BUT YOU'RE BROKE
Please lie to next person in queue that the bank must have made a mistake, then scuttle away pretending not to be embarrassed ....THANKYOU

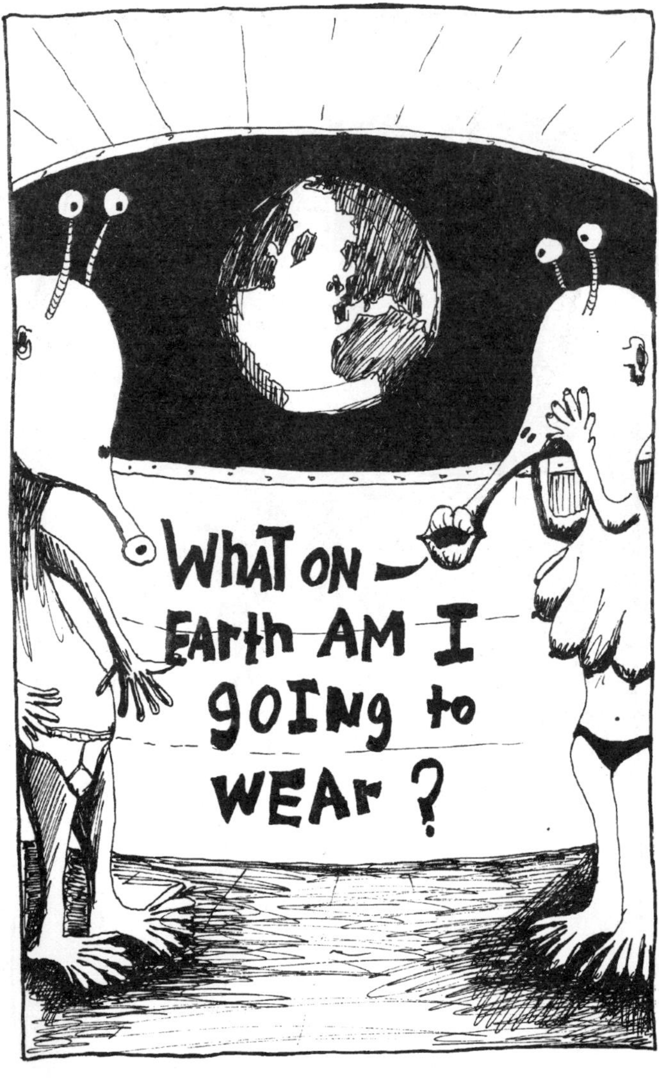
WHAT ON EARTH AM I GOING to WEAR?

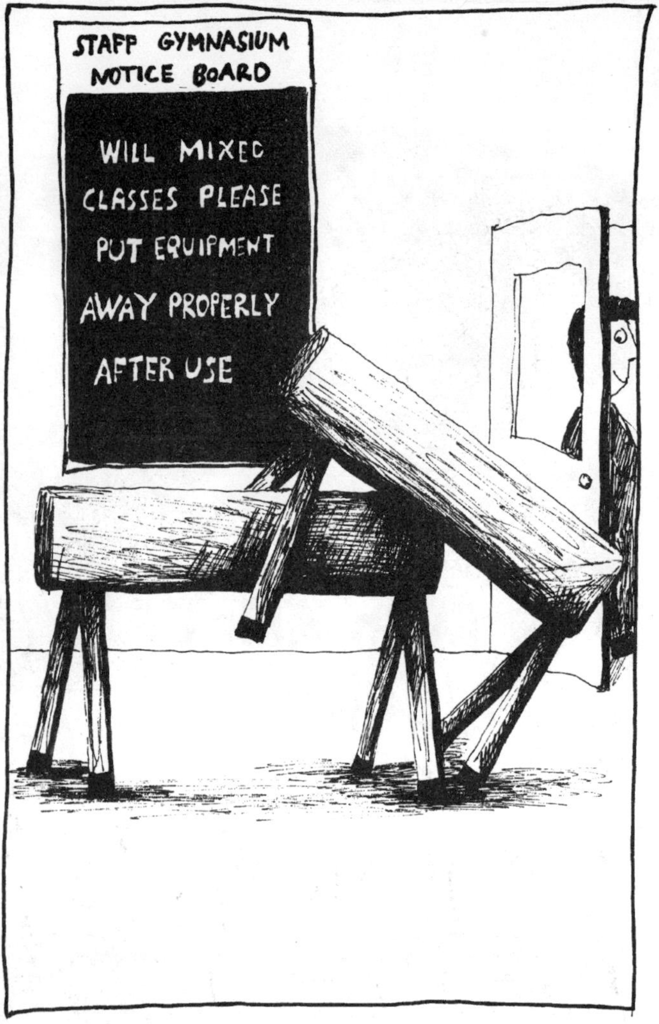
STAFF GYMNASIUM
NOTICE BOARD
WILL MIXED
CLASSES PLEASE
PUT EQUIPMENT
AWAY PROPERLY
AFTER USE

It's the Thought that counts-
_ unless you think that
women prefer BEER
to expensive jewellery

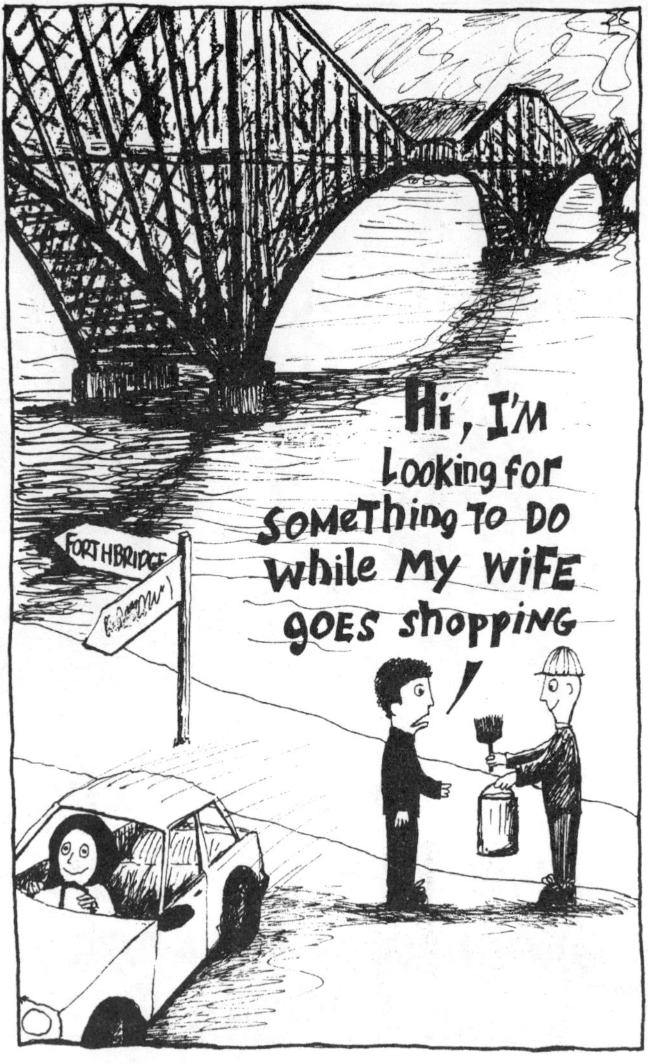
Hi, I'M Looking for SOMEThing TO DO while My WIFE goES shopping
FORTHBRIDGE

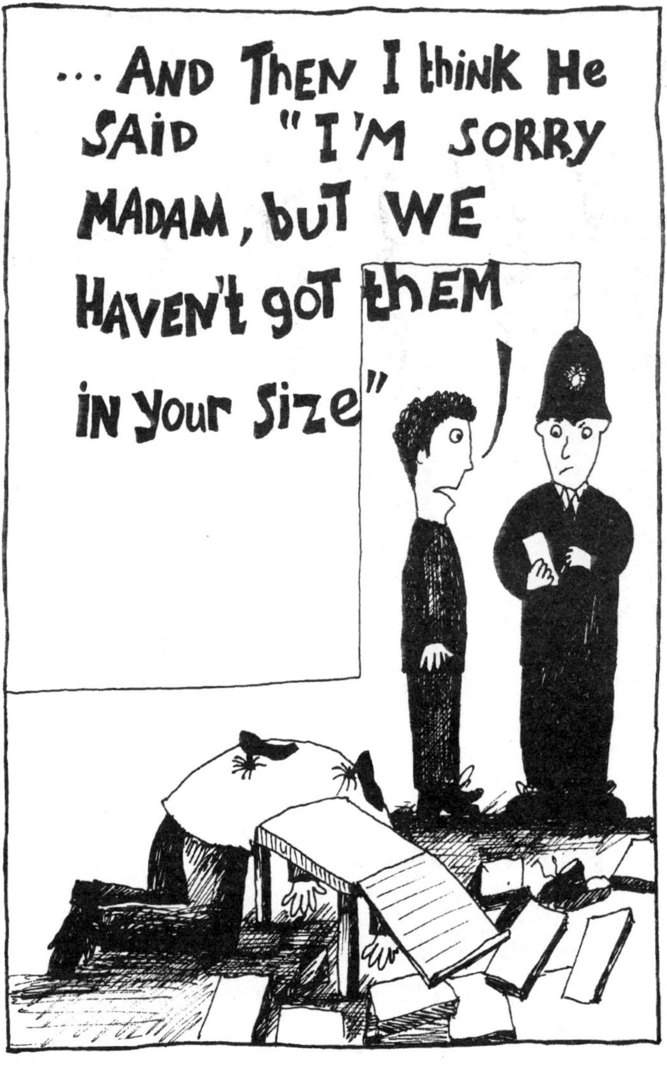
...AND THEN I think HE SAID "I'M SORRY MADAM, but WE HAVEN't got them in your size"

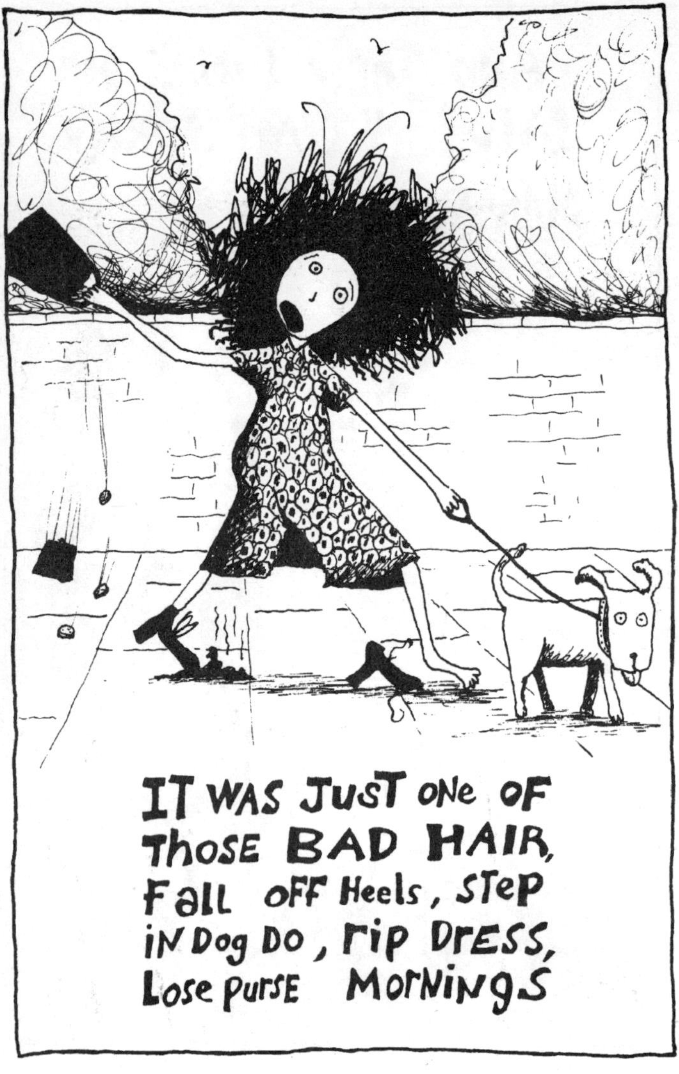
IT WAS JUST ONE OF THOSE BAD HAIR, Fall OFF Heels, STEP iN Dog DO, rip DrESS, Lose purse MorNingS

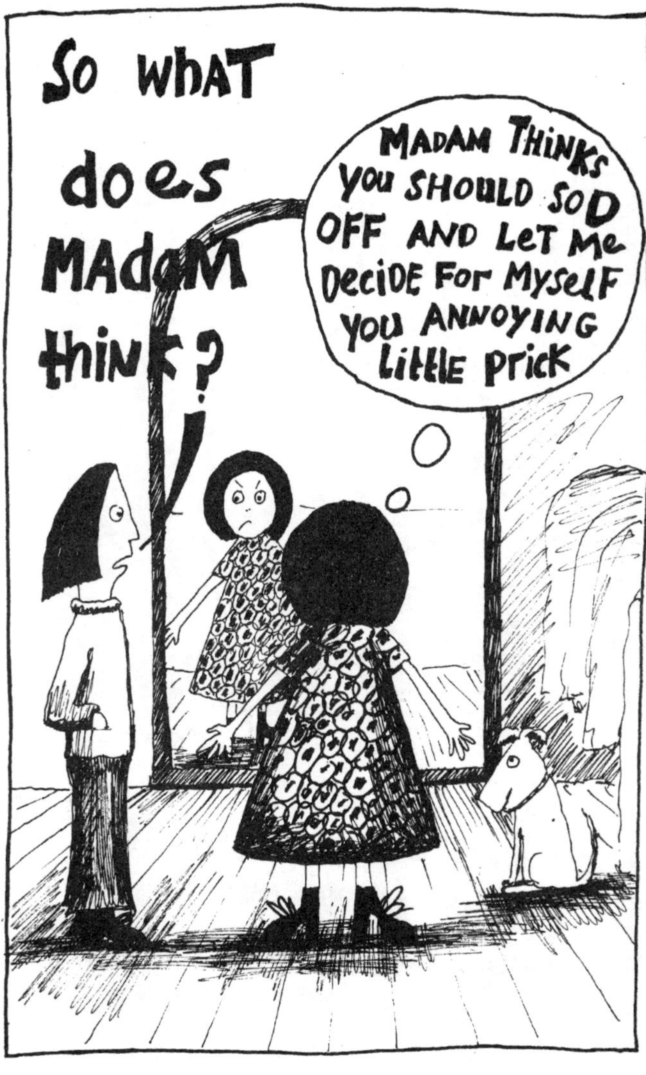
So WHAT does MADAM think?
MADAM THINKS YOU SHOULD SOD OFF AND LET ME DECIDE FOR MYSELF YOU ANNOYING LITTLE PRICK

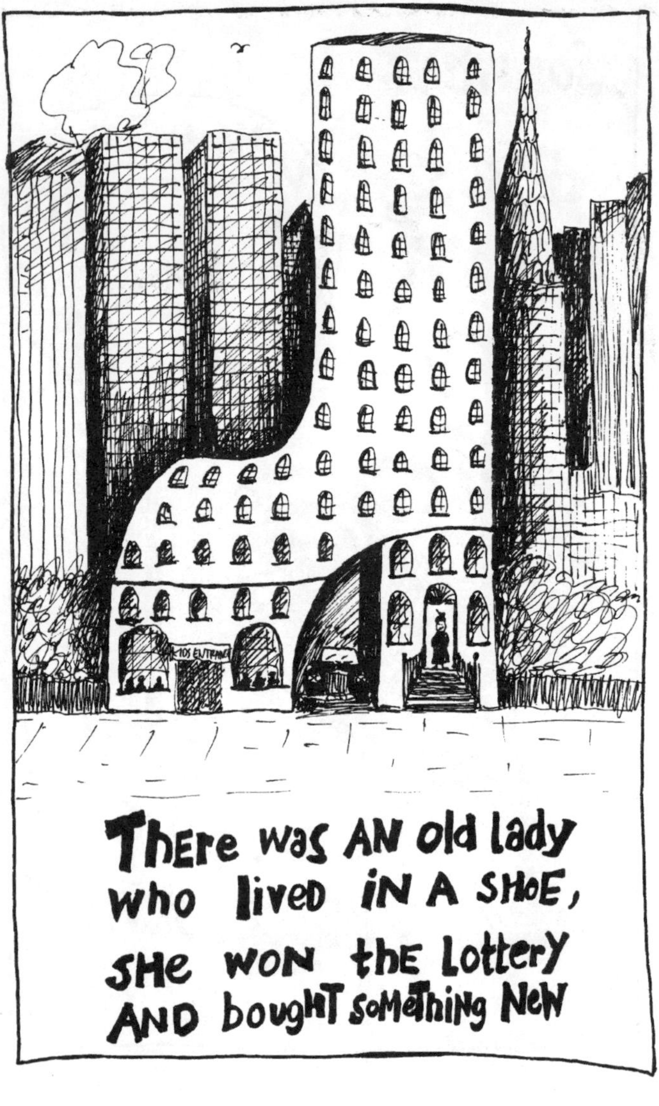
There was AN old lady
who lived IN A SHOE,
SHE WON the Lottery
AND bought something New

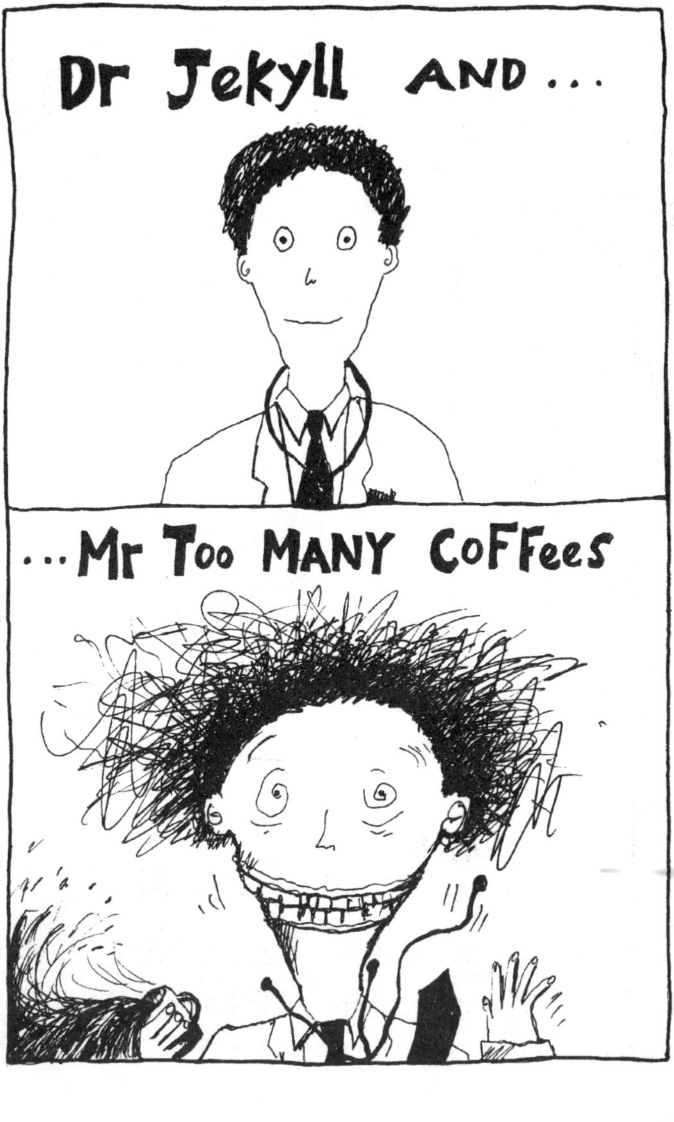
Dr Jekyll AND...
...Mr Too MANY CoFFees

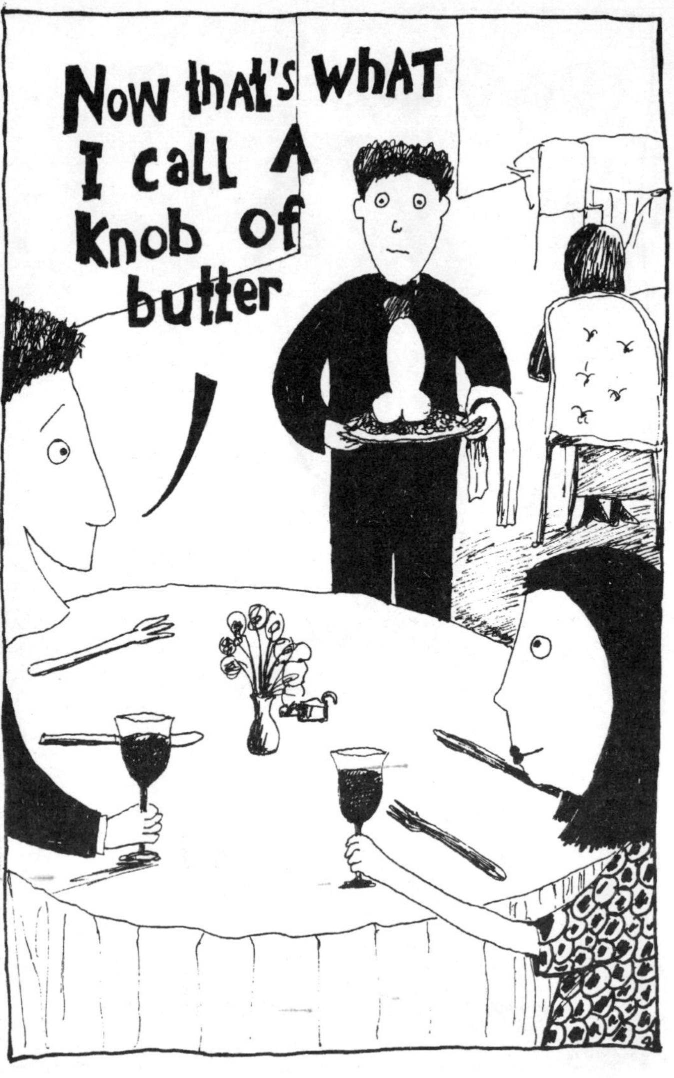
Now that's WHAT I call A knob of butter

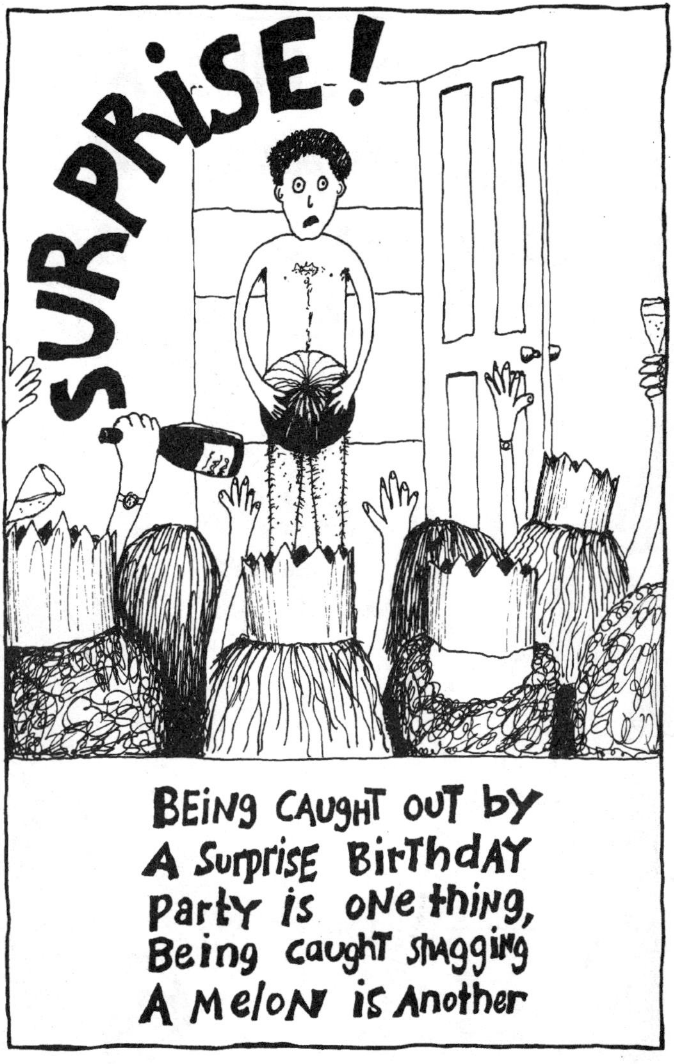
SURPRISE!

BEING CAUGHT OUT BY A SURPRISE BIRTHDAY PARTY IS ONE THING, BEING CAUGHT SHAGGING A MELON IS ANOTHER

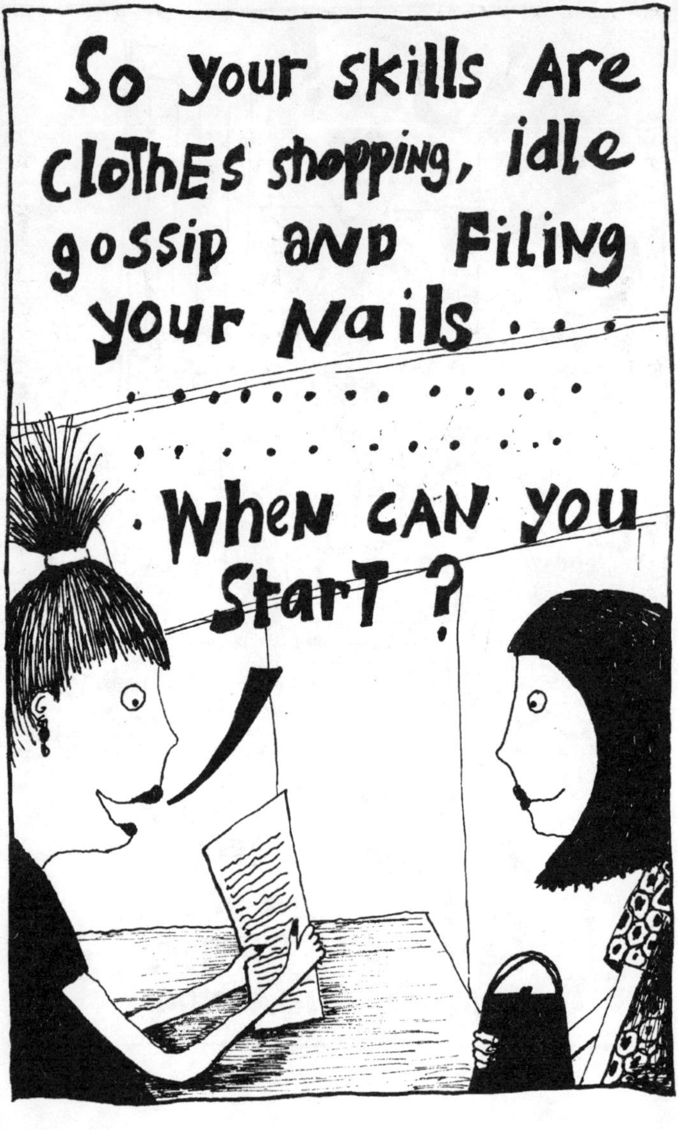
So your skills Are clothes shopping, idle gossip and Filing your Nails . . .
. . . .
When can you Start ?

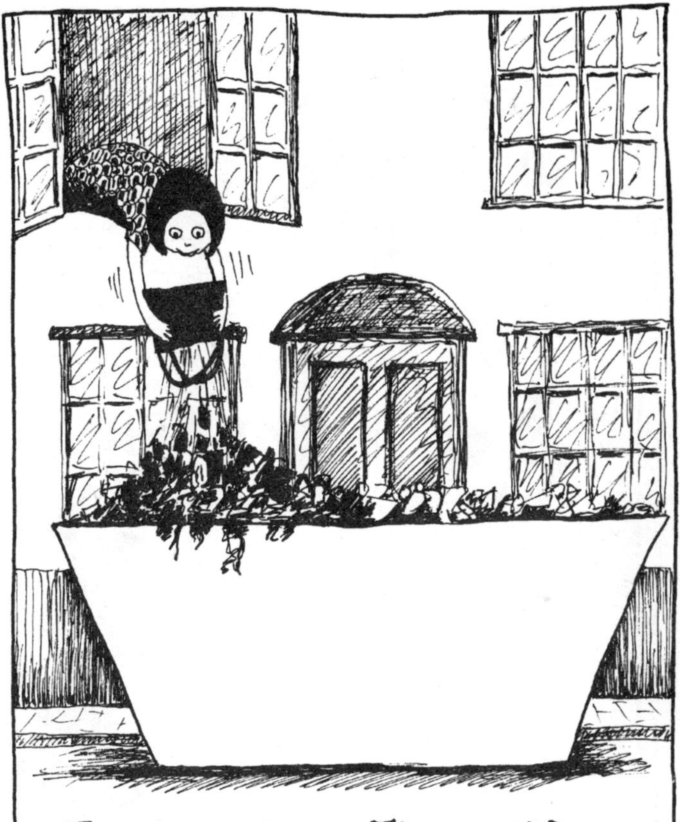
Every so often she
liked to reorganise
her handbag

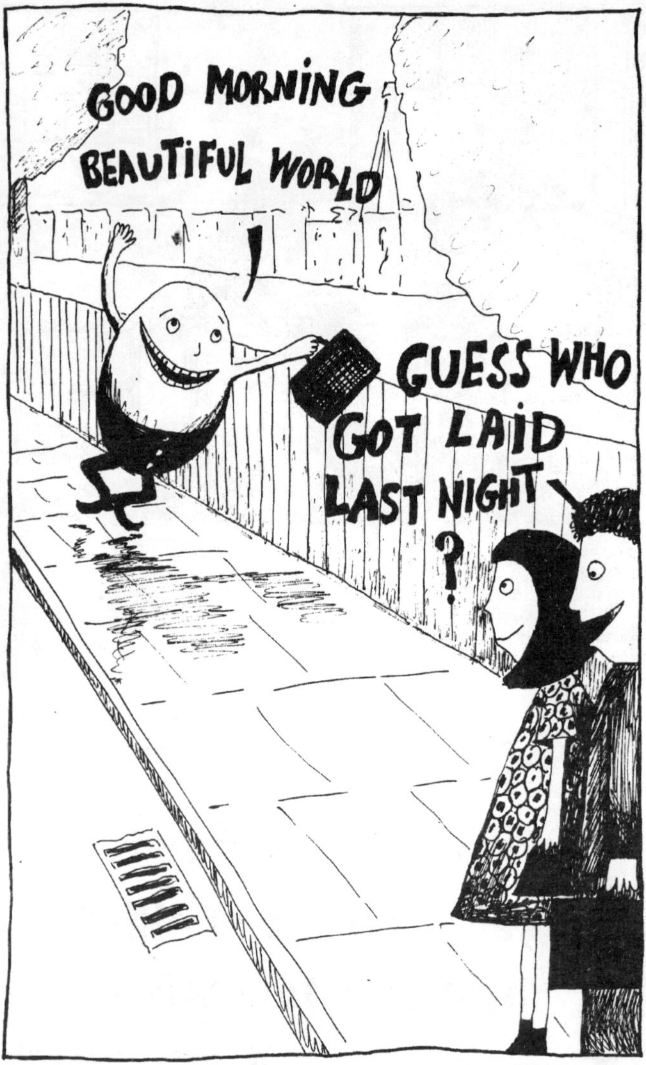
GOOD MORNING
BEAUTIFUL WORLD
!
GUESS WHO
GOT LAID
LAST NIGHT
?

She soon discovered
why Flares and platforms
went out of Fashion
the First time Around

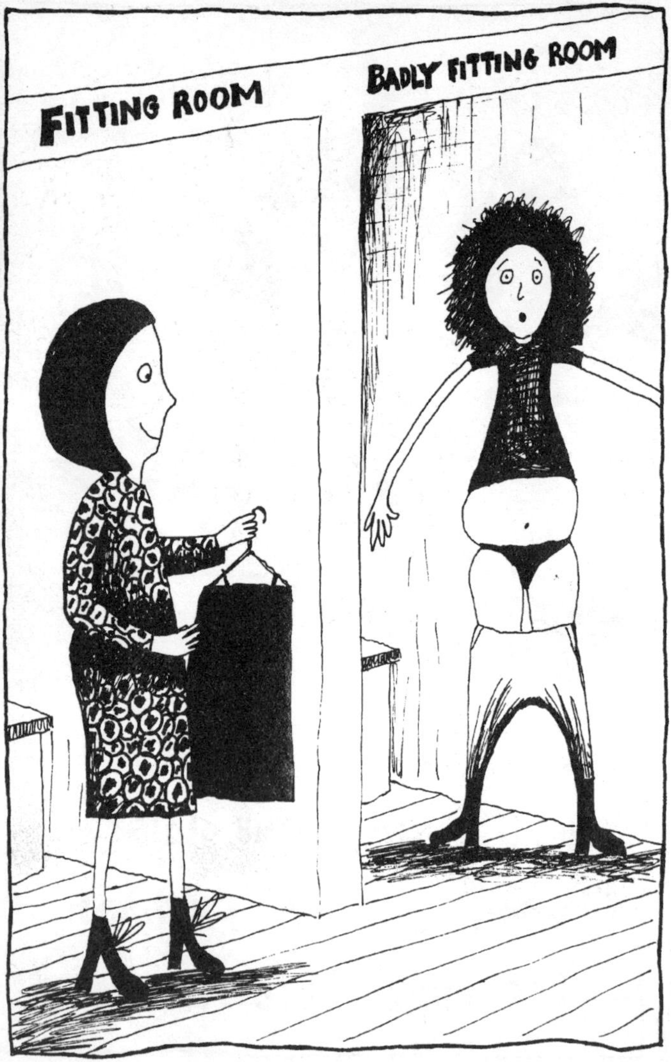
FITTING ROOM
BADLY FITTING ROOM

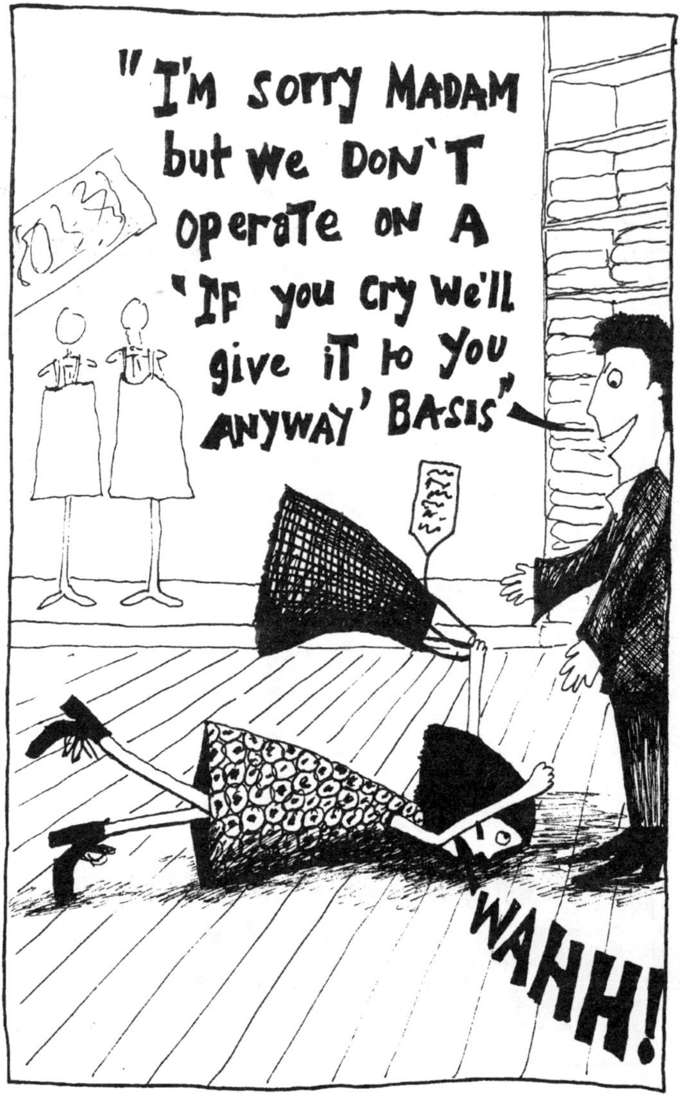
"I'M SORRY MADAM but we DON'T operate ON A 'IF you cry we'll give iT to you ANYWAY' BASIS"
WAHH!

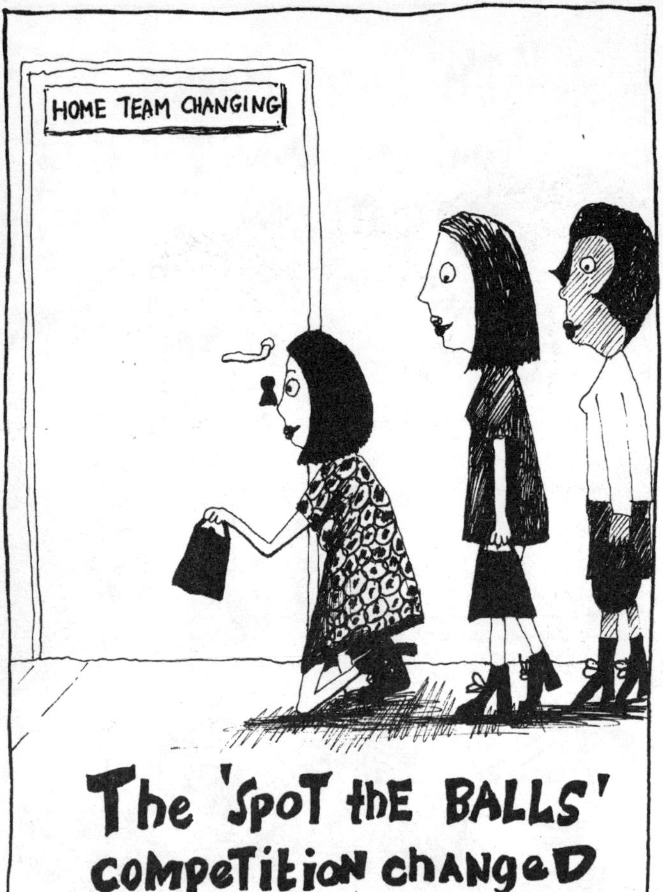
HOME TEAM CHANGING
The 'SPOT THE BALLS' COMPETITION CHANGED THE WAY WOMEN LOOKED AT FOOTBALL FOREVER

Her "I Don't Know What to Wear Today" clothing crisis GOT completely out of HAND

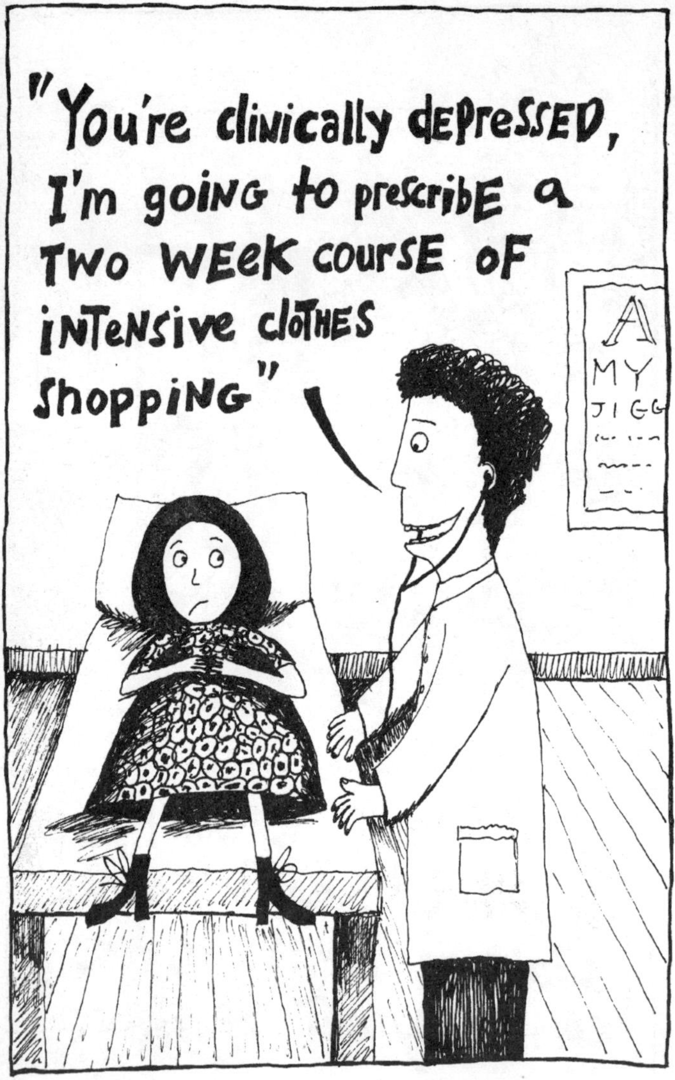
"You're clinically depressed, I'm going to prescribe a two week course of intensive clothes shopping"
A
MY
JIGG

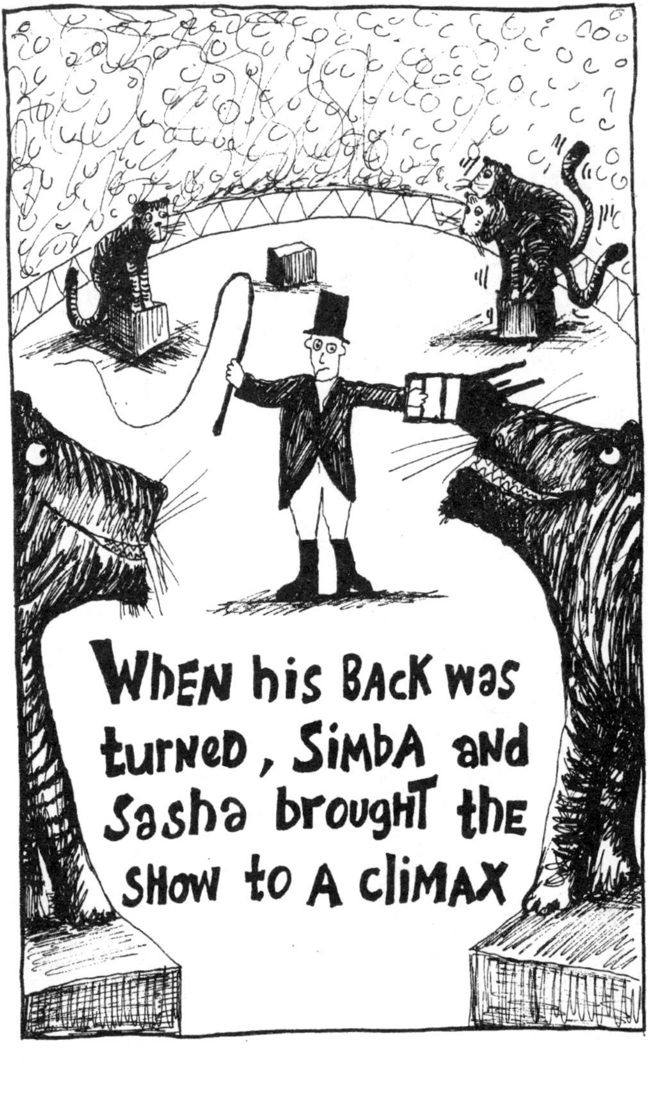
WHEN his BACK was turned, SIMBA and Sasha brought the SHOW to A climax

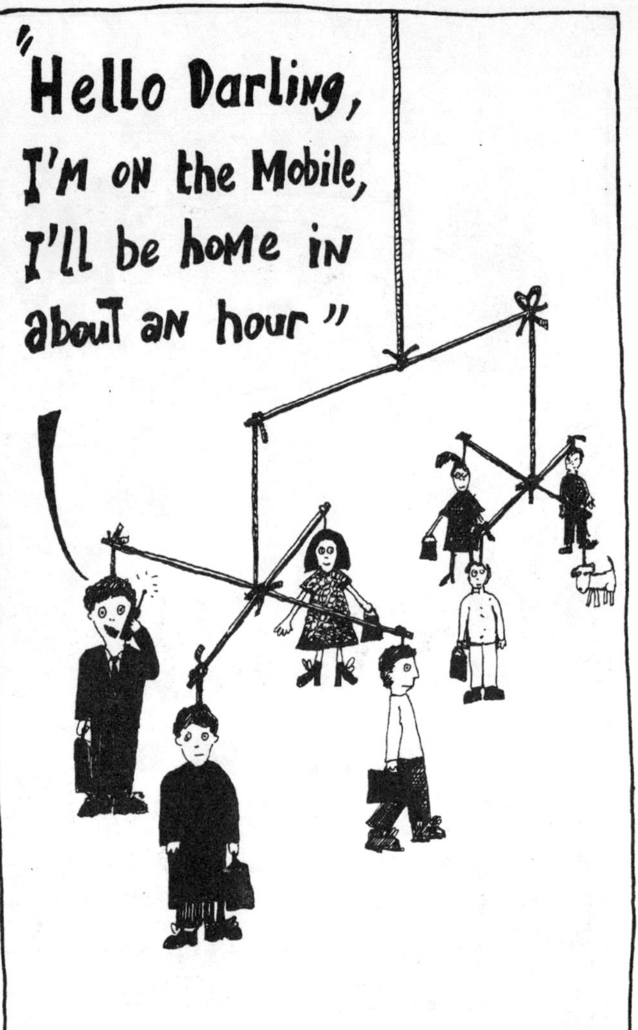
"Hello Darling,
I'm on the Mobile,
I'll be home in
about an hour"

HER DEPICTION OF
FROSTY THE SNOWMAN
SUGGESTED SHE
WAS DREAMING OF
MORE THAN A
WHITE CHRISTMAS

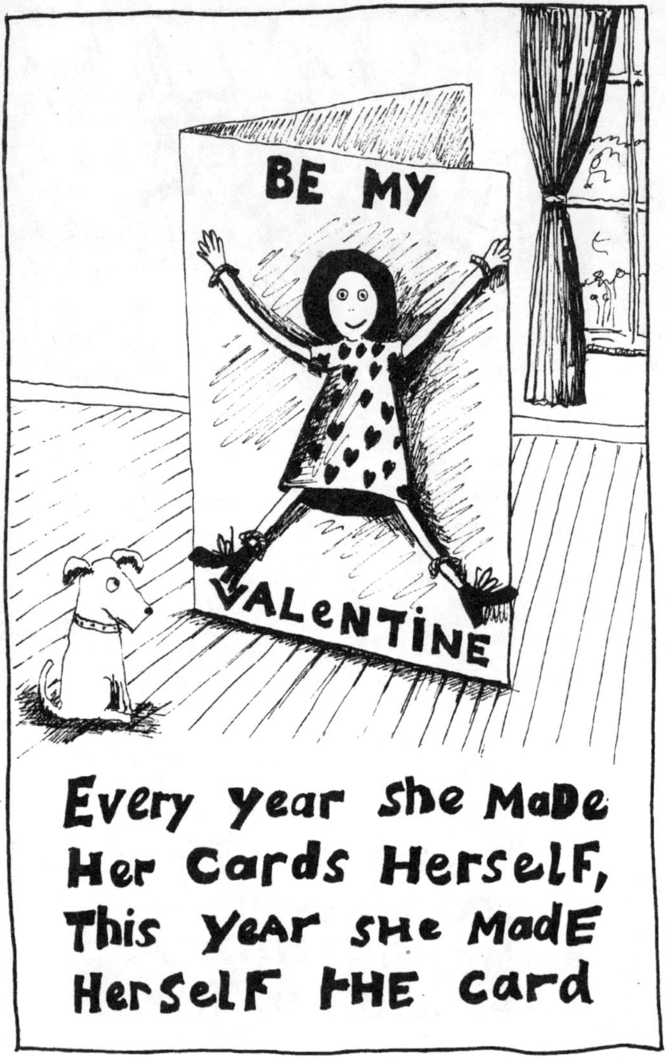
BE MY
VALENTINE
Every year she made
her cards herself,
This year she made
herself the card

THe MosT pAiNFul parT
oF Her surprise VALenTiNe's
BondAge session was THaT
iT TooK pLACE During
MATCH oF THE DAY

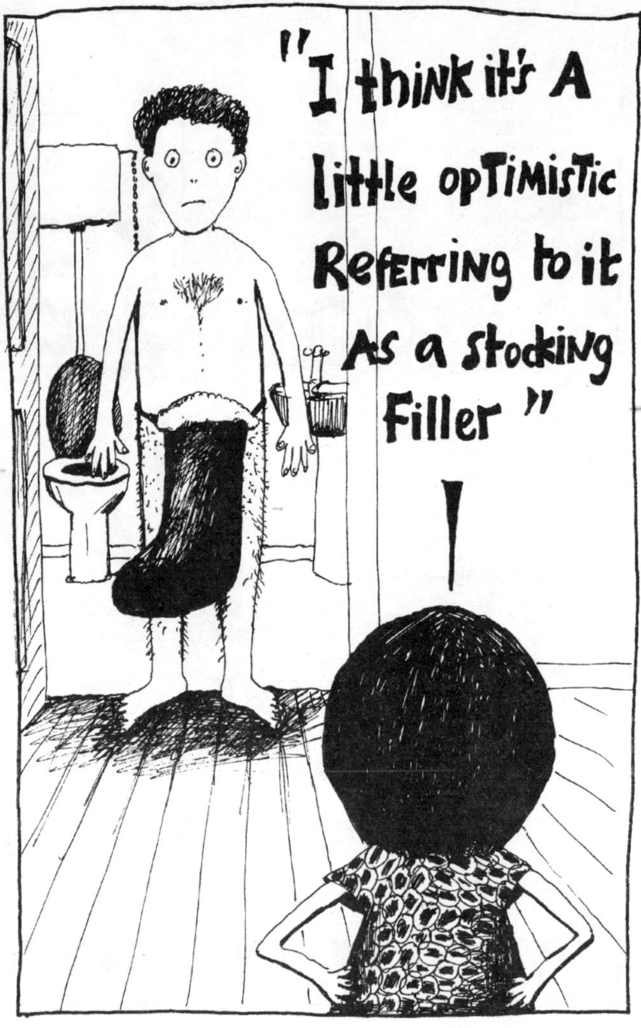
"I think it's A little optimistic Referring to it As a stocking Filler"
!

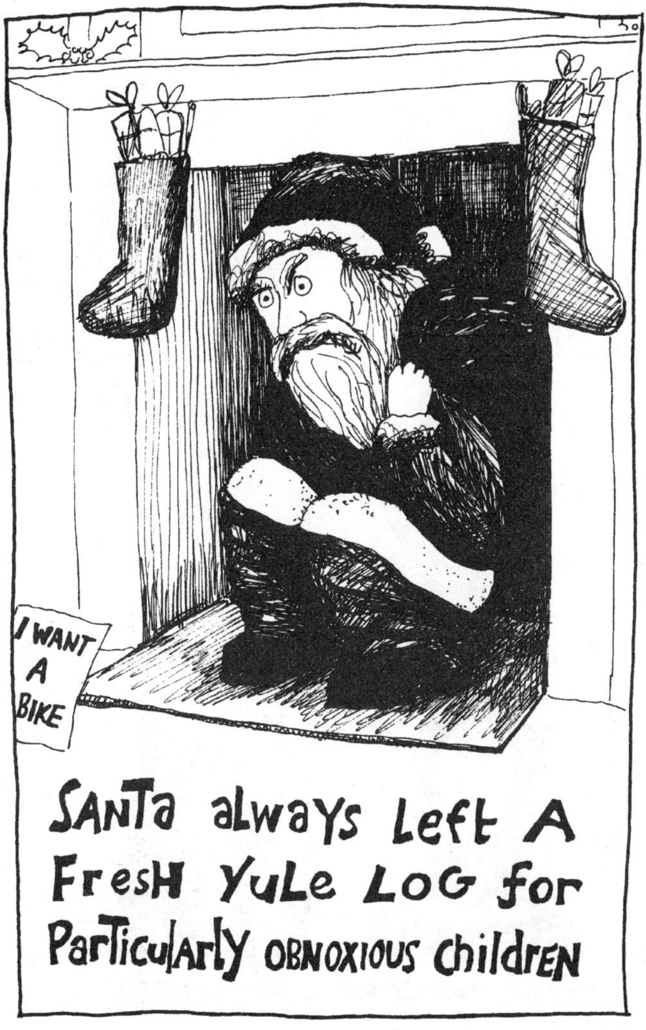
I WANT A BIKE

SANTA always left A FresH YuLe LOG for ParTicularly OBNOXIOUS children

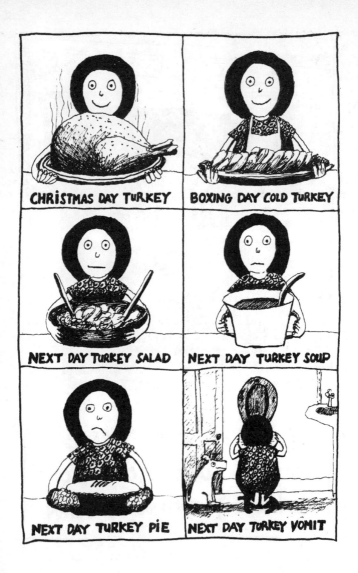

CHRISTMAS DAY TURKEY

BOXING DAY COLD TURKEY

NEXT DAY TURKEY SALAD

NEXT DAY TURKEY SOUP

NEXT DAY TURKEY PIE

NEXT DAY TURKEY VOMIT

IN a desperate Attempt to Get PULLED SHE went to the office party AS A Christmas cracker

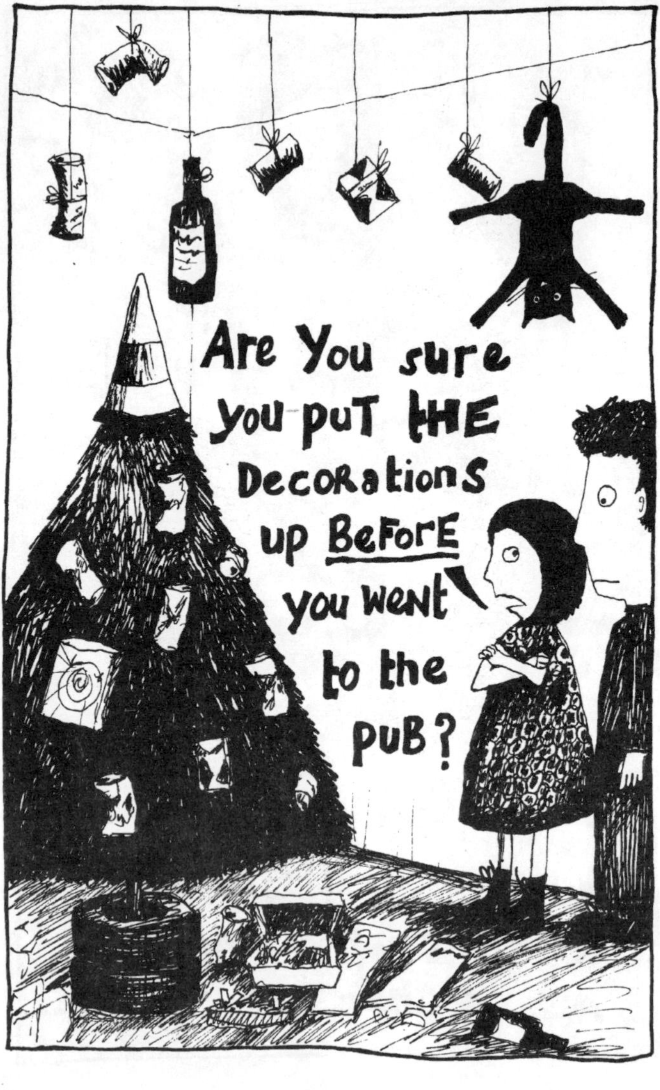
Are You sure you put THE Decorations up BEFORE you went to the pub?

He Discovered THE ZOOM
LENS WAS GREAt For
CLOSE ups but LOUSY aT
getting THE full picture

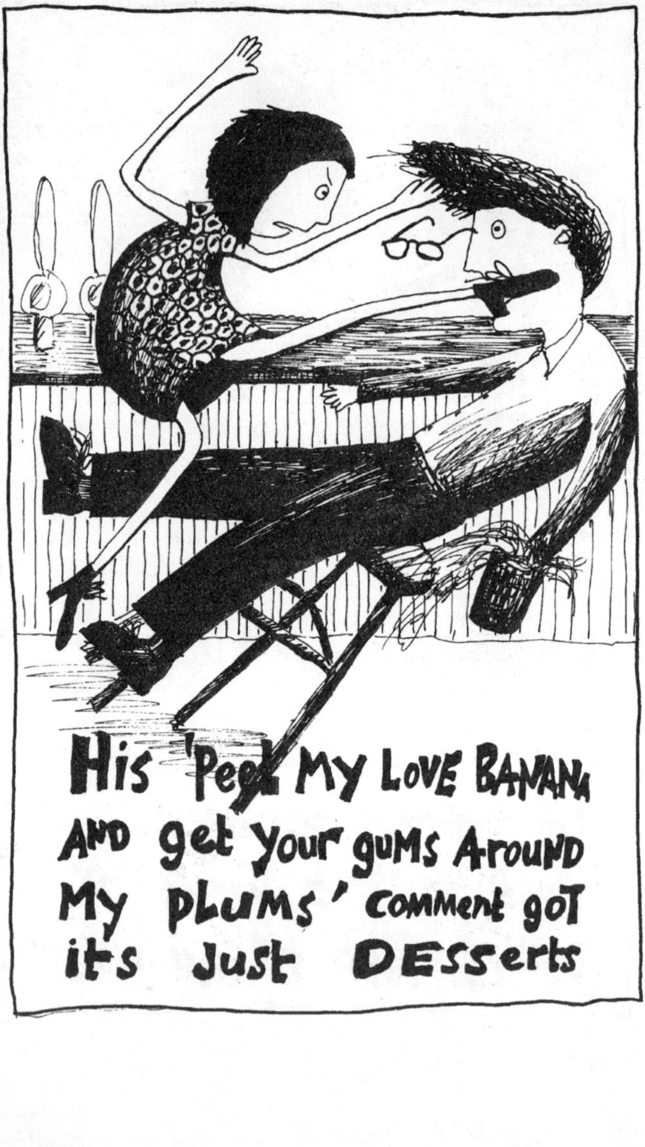
His 'Peel My Love Banana
And get your gums Around
My plums' comment got
its Just DEsserts

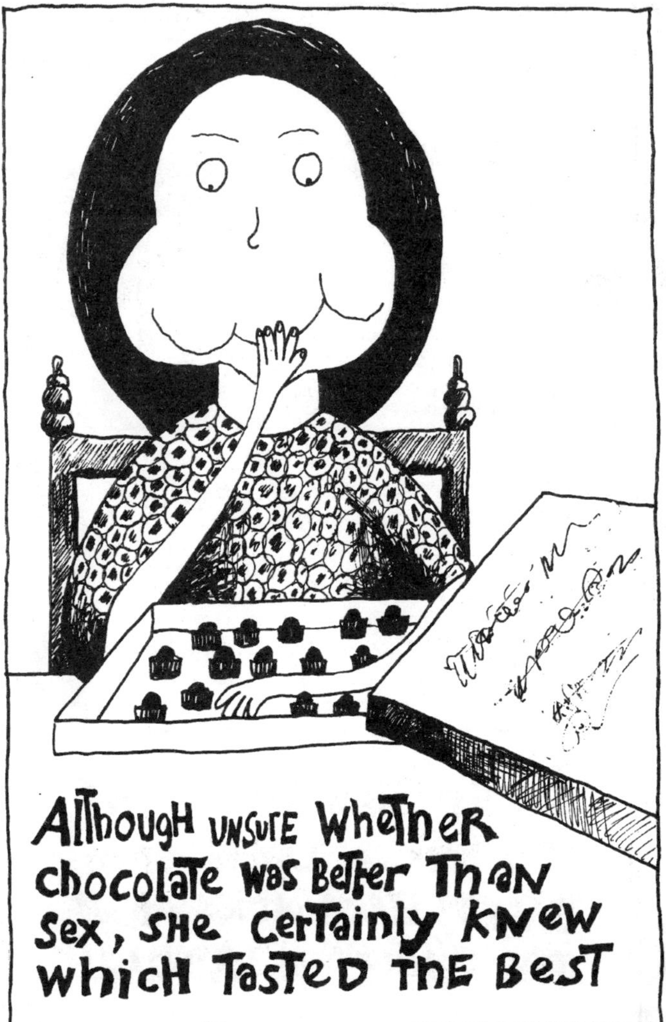
Although unsure whether chocolate was better than sex, she certainly knew which tasted the best

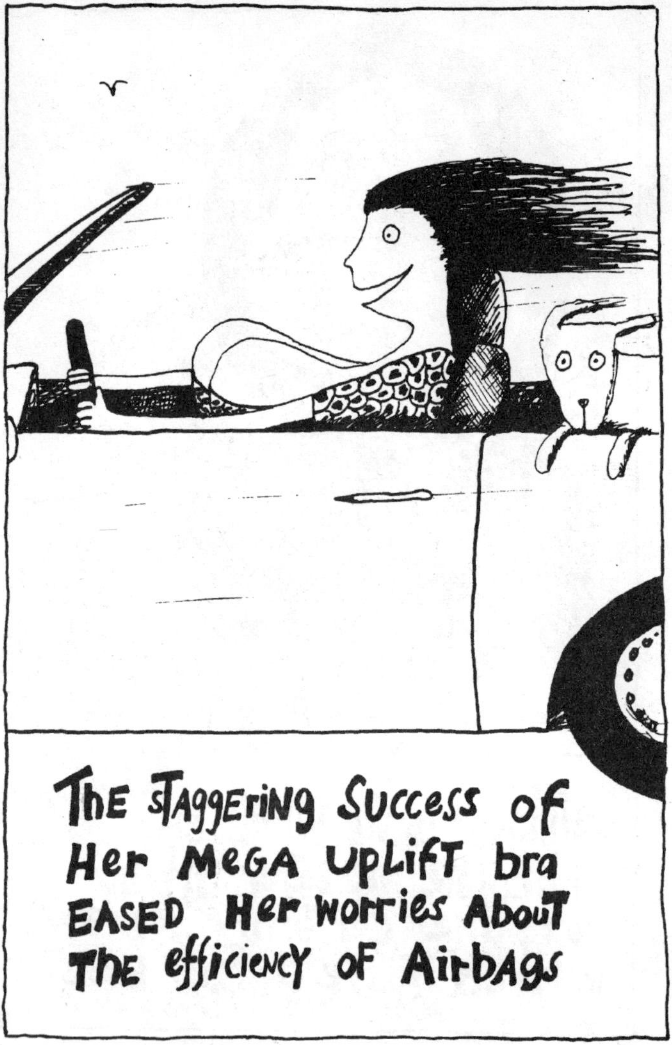
THE STAGGERING SUCCESS OF
HER MEGA UPLIFT bra
EASED HER WORRIES ABOUT
THE EFFICIENCY OF AIR-BAGS

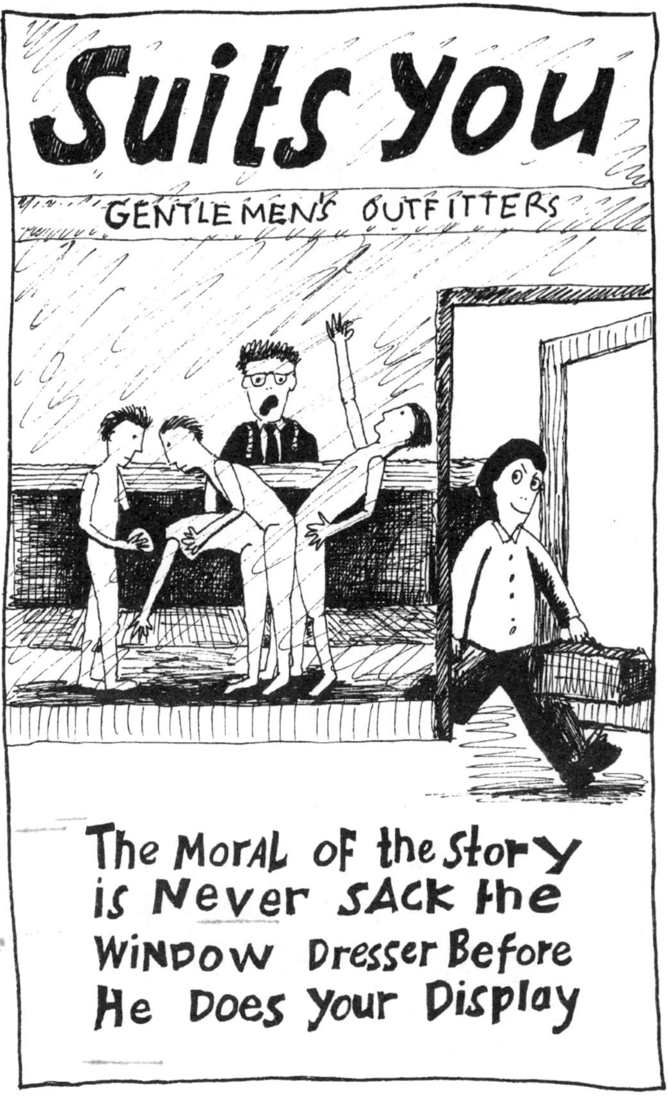
Suits you
GENTLEMEN'S OUTFITTERS
The Moral of the Story is Never SACK the WINDOW Dresser Before He Does Your Display

SHE Discovered HOW
BAd her bAd hair Day
was WHILST trying
ON A New BikiNi

Other illustrated humour titles
published under licence from Paperlink
by Michael O'Mara Books Limited:

Dot on Men
1-85479-348-9

Dot on Top
1-85479-466-3

Santa & Co
1-85479-455-8

If you would like more information,
please contact our UK Sales Department:
Fax: (020) 7622 6956
E-mail: jokes@michaelomarabooks.com